THE GAP IN THE HEDGE

Dispatches from the Extraordinary World of British Gardening

CHARLES ELLIOTT

THE LYONS PRESS

For Carol again

Copyright © 1998 by Charles Elliott

All Rights Reserved. No part of this book may be reproduced in any manner without the express written consent of the publisher, except in the case of brief excerpts in critical reviews and articles. All inquiries should be addressed to: The Lyons Press, 31 West 21 Street, New York, New York 10010.

Printed in the United States of America

10 9 8 7 6 5 4 3 2 1

Design by John Gray

Library of Congress Cataloging-in-Publication Data
Elliott, Charles Aikin, 1930–
    The gap in the hedge : dispatches from the extraordinary world of British gardening / [Charles Elliott].
        p.   cm.
    ISBN 1-55821-680-4 (hardcover)
    1. Gardening—England—Anecdotes.   2. Gardeners—England—Anecdotes.   3. Elliott, Charles Aikin, 1930–.
I. Title.
SB455.E545   1998
635′.0942—dc21   97-35203
                                                                CIP

CONTENTS

Introduction   vii

I   *Local Color*

The English Obsession   3

Gardening and Groundskeeping   8

The Trendy School of Gardening   14

Privacy   19

Old Saws   25

The Wildflower Meadow   31

The "Garden Open" Day   37

II   *Adventures in the Vegetable Kingdom*

The Great Water Lily   45

Invaders   52

The Peripatetic Peony   58

Orphan Seeds   64

Mistletoe   70

The Lost Orchid   76

Nettles   82

III   *Some People*

Miss Willmott   91

The *Finder* Founder   98

Jagadis Chunder Bose   104

Geoff   111

Joseph Rock   118

Canon Ellacombe   125

The Bishop's Garden   131

Reginald Farrer's Last Journey   137

IV Shows and Showplaces

The Hampton Court Palace Flower Show   147

Courson   155

A Dome Away from Home   162

The Show Garden   168

V Antiquarian Pursuits

Water Jokes   179

The Verdant Chicken   186

Pursuing the Picturesque   192

Hosepipes and Hydrophiles   199

Mazes   204

American Weeds   210

INTRODUCTION

❦

I f there appears to be something random, even downright
miscellaneous, about this collection of pieces, be assured
that it is intentional. Gardening is a vast subject, there are
many roads into it, and I have taken particular pleasure in
exploring a variety of approaches, from the historical to the
ecological. In other words, if you don't want to read about
the seventeenth-century garden of the Bishop of Eichstätt,
you'll also find here a meditation on the stinging capabili-
ties of the nettle.

The articles do orbit, loosely to be sure, around one main
theme: gardening in Britain. The British—the English in
particular—have made gardening their national hobby, art
form, obsession. They regard themselves as better at it than
anyone else, and with good reason: their achievements in
style and performance have influenced gardeners all over
the world.

That this influence is sometimes wildly inappropriate
must be admitted—the fellow trying to grow delphiniums in
Anaheim just like Rosemary Verey's needs to have his compost turned—but there's no denying its strength. Logical or
not, the ideal in the minds of gardeners a long long way
from Gloucestershire is still the billowing herbaceous border and polished lawn of the Jekyll-Robinson tradition. I
find this fascinating and slightly appalling. On the other

hand, new ideas are in the air, in England too, and we may live to see the day when gravel, burdock, and Queen Anne's lace finds favor in the land of yew hedges.

My first collection of essays was called *The Transplanted Gardener*, which is the column title under which most of those pieces—and most of those in this book as well—appeared in *Horticulture* magazine. The point was that I had gardened in New England before moving, in 1986, to Britain, where I soon bought a house in the country and started gardening again. This gave me, theoretically at least, a perspective on the English and their horticultural habits. Had I actually known more about gardening—that is, been a more skilled and experienced gardener—I probably would have been able to reach more profound and useful conclusions about, say, what to plant with your *Alstroemeria ligtu* or how to treat Lily Symptomless Virus. As it is, I was side-tracked into something that has been, for me, much more fun: the contemplation of gardening as a social phenomenon. This gave me the latitude to write about botanical explorers, about garden shows, about such extraordinary characters as Reginald Farrer and Ellen Willmott and Jagadis Chunder Bose, about weather sayings and hosepipes and how mistletoe gets planted (by a bird).

As before, I am grateful for having had access to the crammed, deliciously unpredictable stacks of the London Library and to the equally rich (if more specialized) resources of the Royal Horticultural Society's Lindley Library. Each provides an almost unparalleled excuse for wasting a rainy London afternoon. My thanks also to Tom Cooper of *Horticulture*, whose forgiving nature has allowed me to wander around the British gardening scene as I pleased. So far as actual gardening is concerned, which in my case nowadays takes place in Wales (just barely; we are only about a quarter of a mile from the English border), I have—as usual and with undiminished readiness—Carol to thank. We have both been learning, and we both have some way to go. Towerhill Cottage will never be Sissinghurst, but the charms of its garden are increasing season by season, and in the meantime Britain is full of other people's gardens to visit, criticize, envy, and rifle for ideas. Simply being here, in what I've called the world's greatest potting shed, is a pretty good reason for any gardener's gratitude, transplanted or otherwise.

I

Local Color

THE ENGLISH OBSESSION

✤

If I live in England for another dozen years (and I have every intention of doing so), I think I may get a grip on English gardening. But it's a bit like learning a foreign language, or at least a skewed dialect of a language you already know. You can guess at what a word means, but you have to be damned careful about using it. The natives may laugh.

I've often wondered what it is that makes the English such dedicated gardeners. The climate, basically wet and warm, no doubt has something to do with it. (New England, where I used to garden, is called temperate; an English gardener would regard forty degrees of frost as intemperate, and would be right.) Thus plants stay alive, surely a splendid incentive to attempt their cultivation. In America a good many tend to die.

Except for bleak reaches of Scotland and the Welsh mountains, moreover, the British climate has a pleasant consistency. The dazzling swathes of gardening magazines that fill the newsagents' shelves need not concern themselves with climatic charts or special features aimed at West Texas. It's quite enough to advise on scab, recommend a new variety of broad beans, and report the latest auricula championship. Meanwhile, the American gardener is trying vainly to decide whether he lives in Zone 4 (average annual minimum temperature −30° to −20°F) or Zone 5 (worse), because the line on the map is too thick.

Possibly to make up for their insouciance about climate, the British seem to spend a great deal of time worrying about soil. It's either clay (too heavy), sand (too light), or chalk. Chalk is a mystery to Americans (to this American, anyway). Before coming here, I knew chalk only as that white stuff that comes in a stick and is used to write on blackboards. I now know (although not firsthand) that English chalk is a far more significant substance, governing the very character of one's garden. Chalk is *important*. One of these days I will discover whether it is good or bad. So far as I know I have no chalk in my garden in the Welsh Marches, but there is some suspicious-looking sandstone. And I've got plenty of clay.

You don't have to spend much time observing the sociology of English gardening before you begin to notice its class aspects. I'd hesitate to try defining these with any precision—I couldn't do it anyway—but to spot a few of the distinctions you only have to 1) visit the Chelsea Flower Show; 2) read some of the more distinguished and rarified garden writers; 3) take a short tour of back gardens in, say, the middle-class neighborhoods of Tooting or Islington; and 4) watch Friday night gardening television. Britain may be a nation of gardeners, but there's clearly more than one kind.

Perhaps this should come as no surprise to Americans; we have differences too. The retired auto worker in a Detroit suburb with a half-acre of vegetables and a large rototiller hasn't much in common with the lawyer up the road with a collection of tree peonies. But somehow the English seem to be more inclined to draw the lines and keep them drawn. Maybe it's historical. I'm not sure how else to explain the social gap that lies between the hobby of growing giant vegetables for competition purposes and (let us say) Rosemary Verey, the arbiter of gardening taste who advises Prince

Charles on herbaceous matters. The allotments where old gentlemen grow their turnips on the outskirts of British cities might as well exist in another world so far as most of the big-name garden writers are concerned. I can only assume that this is a lingering manifestation of class divisions going a long way back—between workingmen and gentry, Labour and Conservative, posh and nonposh. As an outsider, I hesitate to pursue the matter.

In any case, it's the upper end of the spectrum that obviously fascinates Americans. Ever since A. J. Downing ripped off J. C. Loudon for the Yankee market about 150 years ago, we've been trying with greater or lesser success to ape English gardening style and practice. This is no doubt of a piece with our fondness for Bridesheadiana and other anachronisms, and in practical terms makes about as much sense. Still, the fantasy of English country houses and grand gardens lingers on, and I continue to be amazed by how much of the fantasy still actually exists—the ancient walls, the sweeps of shaved lawn and oak-studded parks, the parterres and well-kept borders on the grounds of old houses. Even when it becomes a bit municipal, or encumbered by National Trust gift shops, the delights of the heritage industry are manifold.

The same has to be said for the absolute—and largely unspoiled—beauty of the English countryside. In the prettiest parts—our own Welsh Marches, for example, or the eastern edges of Dartmoor—there is a richness of natural detail difficult to match anywhere in the world. Surely this has something to do with the way gardening has developed here. It was in England, after all, that (as Horace Walpole famously put it) William Kent "leaped the fence, and saw that all nature was a garden." If Kent had leaped a fence in Hamtramck, I hate to think of what he would have seen. Certainly not a garden.

The fact is that Britain is a small country in amazingly good physical shape. The countryside is variously charming, austere, and impressive, comforted rather than battered by the sea and laced with pleasant rivers. Through some miracle of preservation, much of it remains as lovely as anything in the world. It is, moreover, scaled to human size. It's a garden lover's landscape, and the English garden maker in his suburban quarter-acre or behind a terraced house in London's Fulham district, cutting his own little paradise out of the common stock, has clearly got some rural folk memory in the back of his head.

So nostalgia doubtlessly plays a role in the British obsession with gardening. While it's a truism to say that everybody has country roots somewhere in his or her background, most people here appear to have never gotten over it. Grandees have always considered their country estates their real homes, even when they spent most of their time in London. The rose-draped rural cottage seems to lurk deep and ineradicably in the national psyche, a sort of paradise lost that the right estate agent might still be able to put you onto.

The idealization of country life has had wonderful effects in this country, not least upon the balance sheets of several magazine proprietors. It has also given a healthy boost to gardening. It's no accident that the most popular gardening style of the past century has been the one loosely based upon the writings and designs of Gertrude Jekyll and William Robinson, which grew—at least originally—out of the unsophisticated abundance of cottage gardens. The approach had the multiple attraction of feeling comfortable, of jibing with the dream, and of looking like something even an inexperienced gardener could do. (Many of the latter have since been disabused.)

The British yearning for privacy in their gardens—the lace-curtain mentality transposed to leaves—fits right in here. The recent fashion for garden "rooms"—hedged or walled-off sections that can function independently of the larger design—is a sure sign of the exclusionary tendency. For another, I suppose you might point to the way the classic cottage garden features enormous billows of *big* plants (delphiniums, hollyhocks, and so forth) that the cottage itself can hide behind.

It takes an American a while to get used to it, but having now managed to do so, I'm prepared to admit that British gardeners are probably justified in the air of quiet self-satisfaction they sometimes exhibit. A lot of them—nearly every one, in my severely humbled experience—are really good. Can it possibly be genetic? Looking at the British gardening scene in all its baroque glory, you can't help wondering if something deeper is at work here, some happy sublimation of Churchill's blood, sweat, and tears, or Britannia ruling the waves. What other country could manage to spend £2.6 billion ($4.4 billion) on potting compost and a few other necessaries? What other country could spawn so many millions of hanging baskets of lobelias and pelargoniums in the name of something called "Britain in Bloom"? Could it be that gardening offers the British a sort of psychological pacifier for the end of empire? Or a haven from the crass violence of modern life? Or a way to climb the social ladder (no more allotment, abjure gladioli)?

Enough speculation. It's springtime and all the gardens of the kingdom—ours most certainly included—are overflowing with the only kind of answers that mean anything.

GARDENING AND GROUNDSKEEPING

❧

"Gardening" is a dangerously imprecise term. By that I mean that it covers too many activities, some of them mutually exclusive.

I'll explain. While we both call ourselves gardeners, because we both work in the garden from time to time, Carol and I have quite different approaches to the occupation. She is keen about plants. She can tell you which hebe is which. She knows how to take rose cuttings that thrive. She can tell you where to put a cistus so it doesn't get frosted and why pruning it won't work. A pretty authentic gardener, in fact, although she would insist that she has a lot to learn. I, on the other hand, am at heart a groundskeeper.

The depth of this distinction was forcibly brought home to me last summer when, in the course of clipping off the excess sprouts underneath a clump of lilac, I carefully pruned a prized clematis so thoroughly to the ground that it vanished. It was not a *montana*, either, but a *jackmanii* that Carol had been gently urging into the lilac over the course of five years and was at last about to flower. Now you (and she) should understand that I didn't act the vandal on purpose. It's just that the lilac really needed cleaning up, and when you're crawling around on the ground one sprout may look pretty much like the next, to me at least. Unfortunately it did in this case.

It's all very well to say that these things happen, but they seem to happen to me more often than they should. In fact, they happen often enough to suggest that I ought to question my basic attitude toward vegetation. For example, I have always enjoyed using a string trimmer, in spite of its tendency to vibrate, smoke horribly, and run out of string when the stores are closed. I even see myself something of an artist with it, dashingly swooping within fractions of an inch of the daffodils in the lawn, circling around trees without damaging the bark, edging a path without spraying gravel in my face. (So the odd paperwhite falls victim, so there's a gouge or two along the path, so I happen to back into a nascent mallow and top it—you can't expect to be right *every* time.)

In any case, my point here is not the mistakes I make—everybody does that. The point is the degree to which I, as a typical groundskeeper, am drawn to gardening activities that are only marginally horticultural. Even when growing things are involved, I find myself tidying up. I'm responsible for the vegetable garden (largely because I like to cook and to eat, I suspect), but what I really enjoy is making the rows straight with a stretched string, keeping the beds weeded, and cultivating the soil to keep it loose—and nice to look at.

Mowing is probably the epitome of groundskeeping. I used to do all my own mowing and probably still would except that I was prevailed upon to give employment to a husky fifteen-year-old from the village. I don't begrudge the ten quid—there's much to be said for having the job done before we arrive on Friday afternoon—and it gives me the opportunity to run lightly over the whole thing again, just polishing, as it were, and taking care of those corners and edges which only a fanatic cares about.

I'm glad to say that we also have some coarse mowing to be done, which I tend to save for myself. One section is the orchard, amounting to a quarter of an acre or so, and the other the slightly larger open area sloping away from the house toward our view. Until early May, both of these sections contain wildflowers of varying impressiveness. The orchard has some orchids—early purple orchids, not rare, and confined to a small patch—while the open slope has forget-me-nots (declining as the grass gets to them), daffodils, violets, cow parsley, and a discouraging amount of dock. Mowing the orchard isn't a problem—you just leave the orchids to get on with it, rumbling over everything else with a big twenty-two-inch mower that leaves the cut grass in neat windrows. Very satisfying. Mowing the slope is another matter.

This is where the groundskeeper and the gardener begin to show their true natures. The groundskeeper's instinct is to get out there and lay waste as soon as the grass has grown up to about nine inches and the daffodils have passed their prime. The gardener demurs, noting how nice the slope looks in its spring green, studded with wildflowers. The groundskeeper protests that if we wait any longer the mower won't cut it, it will have to be scythed. The gardener points out that the whole logic of gardening says we are supposed to enjoy growing things, not chopping them down. Why does everything have to be so neat, anyway? At this juncture, the groundskeeper generally backs off and turns to something else, perhaps edging shrub beds with another of his favorite tools, the half-moon spade. Come August, he will finally manage to drive the mower through the grass and the cow parsley, which is now a couple of feet high. The effect will be that of a very bad haircut. This pains him, but the wildflowers will have had their scruffy day in the sun.*

---

*And other plans for the slope are afoot. See p. 31.

Given his attitude, one might accuse the groundskeeper of actual hostility to growing things, but this is not fair. It's just that he is more sensitive than most to one of the great truths about plants. They are essentially aggressive. They want to win. They want to beat out other, weaker, plants, and they want to beat out humans too. Left to their own devices, they will make a mockery of any garden. Brambles and bracken and wild roses will choke a wood, a hedgerow will turn into a narrow forest. In this contest, I'm inclined to favor the human, which naturally calls for a certain amount of mowing, clipping, and chopping.

As you may have gathered by this time, one theme defining the groundskeeper's role in the garden is destruction. Another is construction. By this I do not mean the execution of planting plans à la Gertrude Jekyll, those tempting hypothetical beds filled with labeled cloud or kidney shapes advising us where the hostas or the campanulas or the hybrid phlox are supposed to go. (These always look better on paper, especially in books illustrated with exquisite watercolor paintings of the bed in full bloom. Hard to say why, but ours don't come out that way. Maybe—whisper it—the gardener doesn't know enough.) I'm talking about *real* construction—walls, steps, paving, pergolas, arbors, all sorts of engineering work from moving earth to building birdhouses.

Somehow these activities seem to conflict less with the concerns of the gardener. In fact, one might even note a certain commonality of interest. I recently completed work on a project involving about twenty yards of stone wall, a new ten- by twenty-foot bed filled with two feet of topsoil and compost, a flagged court, a large pergola, and roughly fifteen square yards of cemented stone paving. It took years (enjoyable years), and thinking back I realize that it was all

the gardener's idea in the first place. She quite rightly recognized that roses would be grateful for the new bed, that
the walls would shelter and warm the half-hardy perennials,
and in the long run (i.e., when and if the sun came out some
summer's day), it would be pleasant to have lunch under the
canopy of the foliage covering the pergola. Of course the
canopy of foliage is yet to develop, but that's the gardener's
problem.

The latest scheme, which emerged only last weekend,
had a similar origin. The idea is to build a long rustic fence
six or seven feet high on which roses can be trained. This
will run down one side of a rectangular lawn, properly dividing it from another lawn that is at present set off only by
some dubious lilacs, a telephone pole, a wild plum tree, and
a group of self-seeded ashes. The gardener would love to
plant a whole array of roses here—a couple of red Dublin
Bay, a François Juranville or two, a Bobbie James—making
in effect a wall of roses.

The groundskeeper is delighted. The job will mean, first,
digging out all the lilacs. Then he will have to cut down at
least two of the trees and excavate about a hundred daffodil
bulbs. The rose bed itself will need to be prepared. Then
comes the nicest part: going into the wood to find, cut, and
trim hundreds of feet of poles—ash and oak and larch, probably—with which to build the fence. It will take months of
weekends, given the amount of mowing, hedge-clipping,
string-trimming, edging, pruning, and miscellaneous
groundskeeping that has to be done at the same time.

In the meantime, gardening will go on—cuttings taken,
new plants discussed and purchased, seeds planted and fertilized. There may even be some watering done, unlikely as
that seems now in the rains of April. No doubt the
groundskeeper will be called upon to help from time to

time, digging planting holes, say, and possibly even contemplating where a rather peaked shrub might be moved to give it a better chance. His mind will naturally be occupied by other schemes—clearing a new section of the wood, for example, chainsawing and splitting fallen trees for firewood, building that rose fence—but he is not entirely averse to horticulture in its purer sense, which might be regarded as fortunate. Any garden consisting of more than a window box needs both approaches.

I'm happy to report that a perfect illustration of this convergence of interests appeared last week. The *jackmanii* that the groundskeeper had so carelessly and completely clipped into oblivion last summer has emerged with hugely renewed vigor, sending half a dozen stems racing up into the lilac as if a year's quiet sojourn underground had been just what it wanted. I don't know about the gardener, but I feel better.

THE TRENDY SCHOOL OF GARDENING

❧

It was probably inevitable. *Vogue* (the British edition) has announced that gardens have entered the realm of fashion. "The stereotypical female gardener is no longer a doddery old dear in a battered straw hat bent double over her Gertrude Jekyll border," the magazine declared. "She's just as likely to be a thirty-something high-flier . . . with a plant-buying habit that equals her seasonal outlay on Gucci accessories." Evidence for this development ranges from the circulation increase enjoyed by *Gardens Illustrated*—the posh glossy that can make the bleakest turnip patch look like Villandry—to the number of dinner party discussions devoted to aphids.

Frankly, this doesn't come entirely as a surprise. While I have never spent much time in Gucci-buying circles, it is impossible to avoid noticing how practically everyone you meet here has either been gardening for years, has just started gardening, or is dying to begin. It used to be that gardening was something you did when you outgrew more youthful follies or when the children flew the nest (leaving you with time and possibly even a bit of loose cash on hand). Germaine Greer went so far as to observe that you knew when middle age had arrived when "the hormones turned to horticulture." Now, apparently, it is deeply important for social climbers of all ages to know that ornamental grasses are the *dernier cri* and that Christopher Lloyd looks favorably on red kniphofias.

I'm of two minds about this. On the one hand, I'm suspicious of fads; they don't last, and there are some pretty goofy aspects to this one (a fashion magazine chose to ride the wave by putting some sleek young gardeners on the catwalk as models a few months ago). On the other, it's at least possible that all this attention could help bump British gardening into a new phase, and it is about time for that. We first heard from Gertrude Jekyll rather more than a hundred years ago.

The insidious pull and push of trendiness is already undermining certain long-established English garden icons. For example, the late Derek Jarman, a hero of the avant gardeners whose own eccentric stone, gravel, and driftwood creation was the subject of a popular recent book, heretically dismissed Hidcote, the classic Gloucestershire garden, as "Hideouscote" because it wasn't "shaggy" enough. Next thing you know, they'll be trashing Sissinghurst. (Stop press: they already are. Vita Sackville-West's famous White Garden has been declared obsolete.)

The revolution is, however, a curiously hesitant one. Our cool new gardeners seem broadly respectful of a few abiding fixtures on the British horticultural scene. Christopher Lloyd is admired for pulling out his rose garden at Great Dixter and planting it with a stunning—and stunningly untraditional—array of dahlias, castor oil plants, and bananas. Rosemary Verey, the doyenne of manor house garden design, retains a devoted following, possibly because latter-day yuppies tend to shift into an aspirational mode whenever they see her on television or pick up one of her luscious books. A television series provocatively titled *The English Garden* last fall had Mrs. Verey wandering around some of the most elegant gardens in the kingdom, commenting on plants and talking to the easily envied owners. The programs oozed good taste and conspicuous consumption and went down very well indeed in the right circles.

In view of the fact that Vereyesque skills are in pretty short supply among our new gardeners, it may be just as well that the most recent trends in gardening fashion seem to favor bright and easy. Sarah Raven, a professional florist who decided to create a cutting garden for herself in East Sussex when she found it hard to get the blossoms she wanted, recently published a book about it that has cheered many beginners. Pot marigolds, cornflowers, cosmos, foxgloves, poppies, tulips, dahlias, euphorbias, delphiniums, a few roses, phlox, a shrub or two for foliage and berries—why, anybody could do it! And if things clash—fine. Sarah Raven admits she "likes playing games with gardening—oranges next to punky purples, neon pinks next to fluorescent greens."

Such a freewheeling attitude may be refreshing, but it poses some dangers for our fashion-conscious gardeners, who do not wish to be thought proletarian. Thus a garden guru like D. G. Hessayon is regarded with scorn, in spite of the fact that his twenty-odd how-to books have sold upward of twenty million copies and always top (if not fill) gardening best-seller lists. They are considered to be, well, *downmarket*, and in Britain "downmarket" has a thunderous resonance. Besides, the buzzword these days is "design," which suggests an approach several cuts above such boring matters as air-layering and compost-making and other Hessayon specialities. You have to wonder what will happen if all the students now taking courses at institutions such as Waterperry or the English Gardening School ever emerge as full-blown garden designers. We won't be able to see the trees for the vistas.

Fortunately for the more sophisticated and/or ambitious, the British press is richly furnished with garden columnists, and there are chosen favorites here too. You cannot be too careful when it comes to selecting plants, which have a way of going in and out of fashion faster than flared trousers. Robin Lane Fox, the Oxford polymath who teaches classics, writes learned books, and produces a weekly article for the *Financial Times*, usually strikes the correctly critical note and is closely read by those concerned to know which cyclamen they really must have. He can be savage; luckily, he's usually right.

Closer in age, and possibly in inclination, to England's new gardeners is Dan Pearson, the thirty-two-year-old columnist for the *Sunday Times*, who also had a television show on the BBC last fall. An avowed proponent of strong colors—dahlias and kniphofia and suchlike blowzy plants— he writes well and quite obviously knows what he is talking about. He is also highly telegenic. His recent BBC television series, however, demonstrated about as well as anything I've seen what lies ahead when gardening becomes a fashion event. Relentlessly graphic ridden and gimmicky, aimed at viewers with the attention span of a grasshopper, it was seemingly the unhappy (and unfortunately increasingly common) result of an attempt by television garden show producers to attract the "yoof" market.

Any useful theories about why gardening has suddenly become so popular among young British trendsetters must eventually come back to what sociologists like to call the cash nexus. Britain is at the moment experiencing boom times, with plenty of money for our homegrown Gordon Geckos again after some lean years. Advertising is flooding into gardening magazines, some of it fairly unbelievable (how about a pair of secateurs from Hermes for £270? That's roughly $450. Or a gold-plated set of napkin rings in the form of flower pots?), while fancy catalogues full of equipment nobody needs keep thudding through the mail slot. Of course not every upwardly mobile young gardener can claim much more than a window box or two to delve in, but it's a beginning, and that vicarage in Dorset with ten acres may not be wholly a dream. Besides, a window box is relatively undemanding in terms of labor, and professionals don't come cheap. Time enough for the heavy stuff in middle age.

I really don't mean to sound cynical about this. There's no reason to be upset that gardening is in vogue—or in *Vogue*. Who knows, the *new* Sissinghurst or Stowe may be sprouting its kniphofias even now, watched over by some improbable—and thoroughly trendy—gardener. After all, as the landscape designer Nan Fairbrother writes (quoting someone unnamed but obviously wise), "Gardening is a form of art which everyone, rightly or wrongly, considers to be within their talents." If you end up with no more than a simply super place for Sunday morning Bloody Marys, is that so bad?

PRIVACY

❦

There is a gap in the hedge along our lane. It isn't very big—maybe two or three feet, diminished a bit more by a bramble or two and a fragment of privet. But it's big enough to see through. In fact, people walking along the lane (and quite a few do, possibly four a day on a nice weekend, because we are on a favorite ramblers' route between castles) can gape through the gap and—horrors—*see* us.

To be honest, I don't feel strongly about this. Carol is the one who does. Like most Britons (she's actually Irish, but typically English in this one respect), she is unsettled by gaps in hedges, fences with boards missing, enclosures that fail to enclose. It's a matter of privacy. An Englishman's home may be his castle, but his garden is definitely inside the wall. Strangers peer in at their peril.

Plainly, there's a cultural gap here a good deal bigger than that gap in the hedge (which, I assure you, will be filled this summer). Driving through New England last fall on a visit, I was struck by the oddness of something I had always taken for granted before: the way Americans deliberately avoid shutting themselves and their property in. While you may see a low hedge or shrub bed marking the boundary of someone's houselot, you don't see too many high fences; more likely the driveway will be doing the job. Picket fences hardly count—what could be less excluding visually than a white picket fence?—and the small town and rural ideal seems to be expanses of open lawn, trees, and some foundation plantings around the house. One yard runs right into the next. If you want to see what your neighbor is having for breakfast and you've got binoculars, no problem.

As an American, I'm perfectly comfortable with openness. It may be boring, but I grew up with it and can't get exercised about the lack of privacy it entails. Our national attitude probably has something to do with the pioneer abhorrence of trees and darkness; until they reached the Great Plains, our ancestors' greatest ambition was to lay waste to enough forest to be able to see the sun and plant corn and potatoes. Fences and walls were strictly secondary, and in any case meant for animals. In the same way, building pioneer villages on New England hilltops, instead of in valleys, probably had as much to do with wanting sunlight as with avoiding swamps. But such exposure is anathema to the Englishman.

You can see it in the tight little gardens jammed behind virtually every terrace house in London—fifteen by twenty feet (modest), twenty-five by seventy feet (grand)—bounded by larch board fencing topped by trellis. You can see it in the laurel and rhododendrons hiding the villas of the stockbroker belt. You can see it in the solid seven-foot hedges of privet or hawthorn or yew surrounding more modest properties in the suburbs. Inside these botanical barricades, the English gardener goes his private way, comfortable in the knowledge that his neighbors can't see him, he can't see them, and the entire world—or what he's got of it—is green.

He is not, by the way, working in his "yard." While we are on the subject of significant differences, this is one that probably deserves mention. In Britain (and Ireland too), the word "yard" refers only to the utilitarian area enclosed by the house and its outbuildings—the stables, say, if the house boasts such a thing. It's usually paved. The rest of the surroundings—lawns, shrub and flower beds, even the hedges, for that matter—are "the garden." So when an Englishman talks about his garden, he's talking about the whole works, not just the parts of it where cabbages and petunias are growing. This can be confusing to Americans, and vice versa.

The British compulsion to fortify the garden has led to serious thought about the best way to do it. In city back gardens, the wooden fence seems to be most favored (there isn't room for anything else, and it has the virtue of opacity). Brick walls are lovely, especially when they are two or three hundred years old, but not particularly common as garden boundary walls except in true brick country like Kent; on the grounds of country estates, you are more likely to find brick used to wall enclosures for kitchen gardens and the like. Basically, hedges are the thing.

Those of us who garden in the countryside probably already have hedges, originally planted to keep animals either in or out. Towerhill Cottage has plenty of them, not only the gappy one protecting us from traffic on the lane but others in various stages of dissolution along the edge of the wood and elsewhere. (By "dissolution" I mean achieving its natural destiny as a row of trees knitted together with brush and brambles. This happens automatically within about ten years if you don't keep it sheared.) We have even planted a new hedge, a twenty-foot stretch of *Lonicera nitida* that will form a boundary between the orchard and the lawn and is already two feet high after only eighteen months. I find it hard to believe that this plant is really a honeysuckle, because it does make a nice crisp evergreen hedge, provided you go over it every two or three weeks with clippers (it grows as fast as grass). And you can't see through it.

Gardening books here are full of advice about hedges, what plants to use, and how to train them. I'm rather more concerned about keeping the extremely miscellaneous hedges we've got under control. After all, we're talking about a mixture of holly, privet, elder, ash, hawthorn, and even a rather handsome chunk of yew. But if you are really desperate to shut yourself in, one solution that I've never seen in a gardening book turned up in an article in the London *Times* last year. It seems that a landscape contractor in Devon has figured out a way to transplant an entire living hedge—leaf litter, primroses, rabbits, and all—using a mechanical digger. Keith Banyard figures he can move an existing hedge for £5 ($7.50) a meter, a third the cost of planting a new hedge, fencing it against predators, and tending it for the requisite two years of infancy.

It's conceivable that Banyard's invention could revolutionize the hedge-growing business. Talk about Birnam Wood coming to Dunsinane! Here's instant privacy for five quid a meter, and all green, too. But we have to ask whether it's likely to do anything at all to reduce the sort of conflicts that this British tight-little-island mentality is always giving rise to. Who, for instance, owns the hedge when it's on the property line? Whose responsibility is it to put up a new fence when the old one collapses under its load of *Clematis montana*? What about that next-door laburnum drooping its (poisonous) yellow chains over the children's sandpile? And what about the hedge that grows too *big*?

In its pragmatic way, English common law has gradually over the centuries established ways of settling matters like these by precedent, rather the way it has developed laws to deal with salmon poachers (they are no longer actually hung). Your deed may well specify just exactly who owns the fence, for instance (and if you are uncertain, you can tell by which side the posts are on). You may legally pick the apples from a neighbor's tree if the branch overhangs your garden. Still, such matters frequently end up in court. Newspaper readers have been greatly entertained here lately, for example, by the saga of Mr. Stanton's hedge.

In 1971, Charles Stanton planted a row of small leylandii cypress (×cupressocyparis leylandii) along the boundary fence between his garden and that of Michael Jones in Selly Oak, a suburb of Birmingham. "I didn't notice because they were tiny little things," says Jones, a retired teacher. By 1975, the trees had grown to about ten feet. "In drought summers we were watering them for him and keeping them alive. They looked like a fairy-tale picture. Bloody fools we were."

As Jones described it—in court—the trees had grown to thirty-five feet by 1979. "They were an immense nuisance." For one thing, the Jones's house was only thirty-five feet from the fence line, and winter gales threatened to topple the monsters. For another, the hedge completely excluded sunlight from the garden where the Joneses had been growing prizewinning fuchsias, lobelias, and (dwarf) conifers. Stanton, a retired engineer, agreed to prune the trees to twenty-five feet.

But they grew back, as leylandii will. In 1989, depressed and presumably wan from lack of sunlight, Jones took matters into his own hands, removing what he claims was about five feet from the top of the hedge. "I had to do them gradually," he reported, "because I'm elderly, arthritic, fat, and for that matter bald. When I took one off there was great rage." Stanton called the police.

From here on, everything but the leylandii went downhill. Stanton sprayed Jones with a hose, Jones responded by more dawn raids on the trees. Stanton's son was arrested after a violent encounter with Jones. Stanton sued Jones for trespass. The hedge grew on.

Last fall, following a series of court hearings, an appeal court ruled against Stanton, declaring that the trees constituted a party hedge and Jones was within his rights to attack them. Lady Justice Butler-Sloss went so far as to comment that Jones had "a very nice garden" before pleading with the two men to resolve their differences. Otherwise one or both of them might be bankrupted—court costs were already about £50,000 ($75,000). Stanton, observing that "this is a ridiculous case," said he would consider his next move. Actually, he had already made it: well within his own garden, planted a few yards behind the controversial hedge (now twenty-two feet high and eight feet thick) is a sturdy new row of tiny ×*cupressocyparis leylandii*.

OLD SAWS

✤

I've never lived in a place where people were so concerned about the weather. This is probably the result of never knowing quite what to expect. In America, especially on the East Coast, predictions are pretty dependable; after all, the weather systems have a whole continent to cross (and be examined en route) before they fall upon you. Mistakes occur, of course, but not big ones, and not all that often.

In England, on the other hand, we have to take what we often unexpectedly get. The Meteorological Office—always known simply as the Met Office—has begun offering five-day forecasts in a gingerly way, but in my experience they are fairly useless; presumably only so many information gatherers are floating around out there on the Atlantic, and the weather satellites have apparent limitations. Longer-range forecasts—that it will be an "iron" winter, say, or that we should expect a drought in three months time—are hardly worth bothering about.

In the past, of course, the English lacked even the Met Office to tell them about visibility off Rockall or the likelihood of rain in Suffolk by dawn Wednesday. What they had instead was a vast and baroque system of folk knowledge about the weather, incorporated in axioms and sayings of splendid inconsistency. Americans will recognize some of them: "Red sky in the morning, sailor's [or shepherd's] warning" or "If March comes in like a lion, it will go out like a lamb," both of which are, incidentally, true more often than not. No doubt they were exported to the States centuries ago along with the sack of barley seed and the bundle of apple cuttings. But a lot of others are purely English, possibly because they definitely won't work anywhere else. In lieu of ironclad guarantees from the Met Office, they're still filling in the gaps.

My own favorite source of weather wisdom is Uncle Offa. Each month he produces a column in the *Monmouthshire Beacon and Forest of Dean Gazette*, our local paper, in which he sets forth what we've got to look forward to during the weeks ahead. Offa (in fact a retired army major named Frederick Hingston, who lives a few miles from Monmouth up on the Trellech Ridge) seems to know every old saw, saying, prognosticatory trick, and significant saint's day in the book. He also displays a satisfying lack of gullibility—real discrimination, in fact—about the dependability of what he's purveying.

The only problem is that most of these ancient insights were developed by farmers, for farmers. Gardeners may find them less useful. Last spring, for instance, Offa offered us half a dozen traditional views on May weather and its consequences. Some seemed to agree: "Rain in May brings bread throughout the year" jibes with "A leaky May and a dry June, puts the harvest right in tune." But then "A dry May foretells a wholesome year" and "A wet May spells a dry September." All, as he remarks, very confusing. For what it's worth, I recall that it did rain quite a bit in May and now, in September (after a drought-ridden summer), the rains are beginning again. Offa admits that May is the most difficult month in the year for the soothsayer.

Probably the best-known long-range forecasting day in Britain is St. Swithin's Day, the fifteenth of July. Offa figures that about half the population believes the rhyme tied to it:

> St. Swithin's Day if thou dost rain,
> Full forty days it will remain.
> St. Swithin's Day if thou art fair,
> Full forty days 'twill rain nae mair.

John Gay, the eighteenth-century poet, went along with it when he memorably rewrote the first two lines in *Trivia*:

> If on St. Swithin's feast the welkin lours,
> And every pent house streams with showers,
> Twice twenty days shall clouds their fleeces drain
> And wash the pavement with incessant rain.

Judging from the weather that followed our rainless St. Swithin's this summer, when we all thought it would "rain nae mair," this one seems to have some logic behind it.

Still, there is something rather helpless about long-range predictions like these. Pointed suggestions that you are in for a bad year is cold comfort to us modern gardeners, and an old-time farmer doomed to a rainy haymaking a couple of months hence might well be inclined to give up the whole show and emigrate. Fortunately, for more practical purposes there is traditional counsel on things such as when to expect a late frost, how and when to do your planting, and the kind of weather you might be handed tomorrow morning, rather than a season or two later.

I confess to being slightly baffled by Offa's May planting advice, which is specific in terms of dates but based on zodiac signs, which I've never understood. Anyhow, he says you are supposed to plant "above ground crops" in Taurus (May 1), Cancer (May 5–6), or Libra (May 12–13). Root crops should be sowed during Scorpio (May 14–15) or Capricorn (May 18–19). Another source, however, points out that "Beans should blow before May doth go," which doesn't leave much time. It also observes "Sow beans in mud, they'll grow like wood." This, I know from bitter experience, is true, but my garden is seldom dry enough (or warm enough) for beans before June. As a totally confusing clincher, we have "Who sows in May gets little that way," which I suppose has to be interpreted to mean that May is too late.

Other planting instructions are a bit sounder, including this one in favor of putting out saplings in the fall: "Apples, pears, hawthorn, quick, oak; set them at All-Hallows-Tide (November 1) and command them to prosper; set them at Candlemas (February 2) and intreat them to grow." No less sensible is "This rule in gardening never forget, to sow dry and set wet."

On the frost front, we've got "A mist in March is a frost in May," and "So many fogs in March, so many frosts in May," both of which strike me as overly pessimistic. But Blackthorn Winter—April 11 to 14—is plausible: "Just as the blackthorn is coming into blossom, expect a cold snap." If blackthorn puts out blossoms before the leaves appear, says Offa, watch out even more carefully for a bitter spell. Indeed our *Magnolia soulangiana* took a beating at exactly that time this spring, although I can't tell you whether blossoms or leaves came first on the blackthorn.

The behavior of trees and other plants as a device for predicting weather or choosing planting times has a long and relatively respectable history. According to Eleanor Perényi, author of that delightful book *Green Thoughts*, it even has a scientific sounding name, "phenology." Actually, that term covers all kinds of "naturally recurring phenomena, esp. in relation to climatic conditions" (to quote the *Concise Oxford English Dictionary*), so the thickness of the fur on a woolly bear caterpillar as advance notice of a hard winter is just as phenological as keeping an eye on a so-called "indicator plant." Nevertheless, it is easier to accept the word of a plant, so to speak. Lilac buds, for instance, tend not to open until after the last frost, and such timing ties in with other natural events. Perényi tells how farmers in Montana know that when the lilac blooms, they have ten days to make a cut of alfalfa and eliminate the first brood of alfalfa weevils. Oak trees are exceptionally weather-sensitive organisms, if you believe the folk sayings. In New England, when the oak leaves are the size of a mouse's ear, you go out looking for morels (I did this without luck for years, and still don't know whether to blame the oaks or the morels). Over here oak leaves of that size are supposed to indicate that the ground is warm enough for seeds to germinate.

Perényi is firmly convinced that gardeners ought to pay more attention to this kind of thing, and it does make sense. I'm less convinced that plants have much to tell us—unambiguously—about short-term weather prospects. The oak versus ash observations are a case in point. One classic saying goes: "Oak before ash, sign of a splash; ash before oak, sign of a soak." Translated, this seems to mean that if the oak puts on leaves before the ash, there will be a quick shower and little more, but if the ash leafs first, there will be extended heavy rains. Okay. But then what do we do about this: "If the ash before the oak comes out, There has been, or will be, a drought"?

Is the behavior of other plants any more trustworthy? English tradition says that when goatsbeard (*Tragopogon pratensis*, otherwise known as Johnny-go-to-bed-at-noon) closes up before midday, there is rain in the air; if the petals stay open, the weather is set fair. If you see clover leaves closed and pointing to the sky, "reach for your brolly." And Welsh poppies and rock roses drooping also mean rain. Frankly, much as I would like to be in tune with the cosmos, nosing around the undergrowth to find out whether it is a day for puttying the windows or for staying inside tying flies is just too much trouble. In this case, I'll go with the Met Office.

There remains the question of just how much of this stuff is folk wisdom and how much is a good rhyme. Oddly, the more apocalyptic sayings seem to reflect experience at least as well, or better, than the trivial ones. Offa reports hearing this one in Devon: "If St. Paul's Day [January 25] be fine, expect a good harvest. If it is wet or snowy, expect a famine. If it is windy, expect a war." That has the weary ring of authenticity. On the other hand, "When eager bites the thirsty flea, clouds and rain you'll surely see" hardly washes. I'm tempted to make up my own at that point—or at least to stay tuned to Radio 4 for the 7:55 forecast.

THE WILDFLOWER MEADOW

❧

I'm not particularly looking forward to dealing with my flowery meadow. The grasses are a good three feet high, and the cow parsley was taller until I topped it with a sickle in hopes of discouraging further seed set (cow parsley is a thug). The wildflower count is minimal now, in high summer; even the buttercups seem to have retreated. Still, we will persist. I've booked the giant rotary mower from the tool rental shop in Coleford on the optimistic assumption that it will work better than the ever-jamming sickle-bar cutter I tried last August.

To be honest, the meadow itself is still in the nature of an experiment. It began as an oversight a couple of years ago, when I was prevailed on to leave it until it was out of control, or at least out of the control of my own big twenty-two-inch rotary. It was at that point that I decided to make a virtue of my failing, having been persuaded of the many joys of a wild meadow garden. These included, of course, being in fashion.

If you believe what you read in the papers over here (which have been, incidentally, chockablock with articles on the subject), a wildflower garden in grass is a new departure. Miriam Rothschild, the doyenne of the corn cockle, has even been credited with inventing it. She started one at Ashton in 1970 and "nothing," she says, "has given me more pleasure than the fact that meadow gardening has caught on." Without wishing to minimize her influence—after all, she inspired no less a gardener than Prince Charles to copy her meadow at Highgrove—it has to be said that such spangled spreads have been around a long time. The difference is that they used to just happen, without much direct help from human beings.

Until fairly recently, Britain was blessed with thousands of acres of unimproved meadows—grassland that had never been touched by a drop of pesticide or a granule of artificial fertilizer or reseeded for a good yield of single-species hay. These meadows were rich in wildflowers, which much prefer to grow in poor soil, and don't enjoy being bullied. But since 1945, ninety-seven percent of such meadows have disappeared, victims (or, if you are a modern farmer, beneficiaries) of the new practices intended to increase output. The winner, botanically speaking, has been the grasses. The losers include twenty-two species of wildflowers that have actually become extinct, as well as a vast amount of rural diversity. "The new fields," says one despairing ecologist, "are about as rich in wildlife as a car park."

Nostalgia for this vanishing treasure is one impetus behind what garden expert Stephen Lacy has called "the most innovative theme in planting design . . . since Gertrude Jekyll." But there are doubtlessly others, in view of the fact that much of the most influential work in the style is being done in Germany and Holland, not countries noted for ancient meadowland. Similarly, recent American interest in creating—or recreating—prairie gardens, featuring such plants as wild hyacinth, milkweed, and goldenrod (and burning them off periodically), is unlikely to be the result of a yearning for a return to the days before the sod-busters. In both cases, the motive seems to be a new "green" appreciation for the beauty of wild plants and for growing them in a more natural fashion.

Of course, "growing them in a more natural fashion" is the rub. There's still a pecking order, even in the world of yellow rattle and wild carrot. A hundred years ago, William Robinson could nonchalantly recommend in *The Wild Garden* that "All planting in the grass should be in natural groups or prettily fringed colonies, growing to and from as they like after planting," but anyone who has attempted making plantings in grass knows that "grouping" is only the beginning of the battle. The real problem is preventing the plants you want from being swamped by those you don't want.

There is some difference of opinion about which plants you should want, when it comes to that, or just how wild the garden should be. In ordinary gardening (if I may so term it), suitability is usually a matter of hardiness or design effect or possibly taste. In wild gardening it seems to be a question of how far you want to go. You can put some daffodils and crocuses in your lawn and stop mowing for a while, or you can go the whole hog and cultivate nettles. Most wild gardens are somewhere in between, and the extraordinary thing is how varied, and strangely exciting and beautiful, the permutations can be.

To a greater extent than usual, the wild gardener is at the mercy of his local conditions, as a recent international symposium at Kew made clear. Attempting a prairie garden in Shropshire just isn't on. Damp and cool summers over here mean that such tough American species as rudbeckias and the like fall prey to snails and slugs, while such English delicacies as wild orchids and cowslips would simply burn up in an Illinois summer. Grasses, too, tend to be extra vigorous in the British climate, making it necessary to concentrate on clump-forming species rather than those that spread by underground runners.

Anyone foolish enough to regard wild gardening as laborsaving, particularly in the creation stage, was also roundly disabused by speakers at the Kew symposium. Initial ground preparation can be heroic—stripping off the topsoil, for a start, and possibly keeping the ground barren for a year or two, blasting unwanted survivors with Roundup whenever they have the temerity to show their heads. Only after that can seeding take place, with a carefully balanced mixture of appropriate species. Weeding is still necessary (less so if you find thistles "dramatic," as one wild gardener defensively claimed to do), and if you want anything special you may have to insert plugs of already-started plants. Then there is the mowing and—of first importance—the raking, which if neglected will add nutrients to the soil as the cut grass rots down.

As far as I know, my small patch of meadow has never been artificially fertilized or seeded, but it is nevertheless home to some of the most powerful and aggressive grass I have ever seen. Without any doubt, the earth there is wonderfully, hopelessly, rich, and I suspect that short of bulldozing the topsoil—which is not in the picture—I can do little about it. Six or eight years ago, when I first cleared the area of a scurf of brambles and brush, almost no grass was in evidence. The first plants to emerge in the spring were forget-me-nots, which flourished with huge vigor, and a few long-neglected daffodils. But as the years passed and I mowed every month or so, grass began to get the upper hand. The forget-me-nots retreated to the wood's edge. The daffodils, saved by their good timing, continued to make a show before the grass got high. But by July, most of what you saw were the plumes of rye, timothy (*Phleum pratense*), and annual meadow grass (*Poa annua*), along with the towering white plates of burnet saxifrage (*Pimpinella saxifraga*), cow parsley (*Anthriscus sylvestris*), and hogweed. This is still the case, but there has been some improvement.

Late last summer, a friend with a meadow much bigger and more advanced than mine—he has even produced a wild gladiolus (G. *illyricus*) among other unlikely treasures—told me about a dodge he tried on the suggestion of a wild-gardening neighbor. An abandoned churchyard was about to be mowed for the first time in years. He collected sackfuls of the cut hay and spread it in his own meadow for the sake of the seed. And indeed quite a few new species appeared the next year. He offered me a few shopping bags full of his own recent cutting, which I took home and scattered.

This spring, among the daffodils, we had a splendid display of lady's smock (*Cardamine pratensis*), lovely little pale lilac-to-white blossoms that kept appearing for close to a month. Purple knapweed (*Centaurea nigra*) has emerged and more tall meadow buttercups (*Ranunculus acris*) than ever before. Even the grass seems more graceful. To a certain (admittedly small) degree, it is already a wildflower meadow, although perhaps not one to meet with the approval of the experts at Kew.

On the principle of letting the seeds ripen before I chop everything down, the first mowing now takes place in August, with a second mowing as late as possible in the fall to leave the grass short over the winter. There doesn't seem to be much unanimity among the experts as to the correct timing here—Christopher Lloyd mows first in early July, for example, and then again twice more before winter, but he is operating on the same principle of giving annuals time to shed their seed and making sure the turf is low for spring flowers.

The real question, and one for which I don't expect to have an answer for several years yet, is whether my meadow will achieve—on its own—an equilibrium that includes a fair number of wildflowers. I'm reluctant to tinker. After all, what's natural about a natural garden that wants more tending than a bed full of hybrid tea roses? Such balance can occur. As the garden writer Mary Keen has noted, the untended margins of small English roads and lanes often harbor wonderful collections of native plants, quite without human assistance. She mentions cowslips and orchids, followed by meadow cranesbill and mullein; in our neighborhood it's the same, plus purple loosestrife, wild astilbe, bird's-foot trefoil, and hawkweed. On the other hand, she mourns the fact that her hopefully launched wild garden is at the moment a monoculture of oxeye daisies and grass, the clustered bellflowers and lady's bedstraw she planted having vanished. Could it be that nature is telling her—and us— something?

THE "GARDEN OPEN" DAY

※

I have always been deeply hesitant, in this land of viciously competitive gardeners, to claim anything special for the gardens of Towerhill Cottage. Some years ago, fresh to the wonders of the Yellow Book, I briefly speculated on the possibility of getting our garden listed in this exclusive compendium of private gardens open to the public on certain days for charity. I even went so far as to add up the number of minutes of "horticultural interest" it might supply. Unofficially, the National Garden Scheme, which publishes the Yellow Book, demands forty-five minutes of high-class amusement. Needless to say, our garden didn't make it and probably still won't.

But in the hierarchy of British gardening achievement, there are lesser pinnacles than the Yellow Book. Last week, in a spirit of something that until the very last minute looked a lot like hubris, we claimed one of them for Towerhill Cottage. We had a public GARDEN OPEN day to benefit the Skenfrith Village Hall Fund.

At this point, there are a couple of things that need explaining. First, the fund.

Skenfrith is a very tiny village indeed, with one pub, no shop (or post office), and no businesses except for a flour mill driven by a waterwheel. The castle, although an attractive ruin, has been distinctly nonfunctional for at least six hundred years. As a focal point for local activities, therefore, the village hall is of some importance, but it happens to be seriously in need of major repairs—roughly £50,000 worth, to be precise. Thanks to the initiative of our neighbor Alan Jones, nearly half of this sum has been secured with a grant from Britain's National Lottery, but to get it the village must match it from its own modest resources. The result has been a splendid efflorescence of jumble sales, car boot sales, auctions, fêtes, duck races in the river (plastic ducks), and anything else anyone can think of that might raise some money. Our GARDEN OPEN day fell in the last category.

Now there is nothing particularly arcane about a GARDEN OPEN day, when you pay to visit somebody's garden—this happens in America too (and, for all I know, in Brazil and Uzbekistan). The protocol of a British GARDEN OPEN day, however, is highly developed. To meet expectations, it has to have certain features, among which the garden itself plays a large but not necessarily dominant role. As I have learned (partly to my relief), at least as important as the quality of the buddleias is the quality of the tea and cakes on offer and the number, price, and variety of the potted plants for sale on the plant stand.

It was about the middle of June a year ago that we realized that our garden was finally beginning to look pretty good and might even measure up to a GARDEN OPEN day. Carol and I had been working on it for ten years by then in an unfocused way, starting mostly from scratch—only a couple of beds, now mainly replanted, survived from those that were there when we arrived. Lawns had been extended to take in overgrown areas, hedges laid and cut, the orchard cleaned up, masses of purple *Rhododendron ponticum* grubbed out, new trees and shrubs planted. The sunken garden with a flagged floor and stone retaining walls was complete; a pergola now bore swags of grapes, roses, and clematis. We had just decided to create a large new bed—some fifteen by fifty feet—which was bound to appear anything but mature for a year or two yet. But the Village Hall Fund needed money. With mild trepidation, we volunteered. Our GARDEN OPEN day was set for the fifteenth of June, a Sunday, and a time when (at least in theory) the garden would be at its very peak.

It was an unusual spring. After a fairly wet March, April and the first half of May had been, for Britain, dry as a bone. This made it possible to dig the new bed earlier than expected, which was a plus, but then it dried out excessively into ceramic-like lumps. We planted it anyway, in hopes that it would not look too empty by June—some dahlia tubers ("Bishop of Llandaff" and a few others), shrubs (buddleias, a *Cornus controversa*, several parahebes, and fuchsias), a rose bush or two, a lot of pathetically small seedlings that I had started hopefully on a windowsill (*Nicotiana sylvestris*, cosmos, flax, *Salvia × superba*, campanulas, catmint), and a few annuals seeded directly (more cosmos, *Limnanthes*, larkspur). In mid-May the heavens opened, battering my new plantings and leaving the soil—once it dried again—covered by a half-inch-thick crust of hardened clay.

But other preparations were more promising. Marcus, the local boy on whom I depended for the mowing, got the rough grass in the orchard in shape with the big mower, only briefly delayed by the need to extract the stump of an old apple tree that broke off last winter in a gale. The meadow required no work; Alan Jones's sheep, as usual, took care of that. Carol tirelessly pruned shrubs and cleaned beds and clipped the bay hedge with secateurs. I worked on the vegetable patches, ran the gas-powered clippers over the other hedges (a process that can require holding an eight-pound machine at arm's length above your head for twenty painful minutes at a stretch), and generally questioned the wisdom of the whole undertaking. All this happened on weekends.

As the GARDEN OPEN day approached, it began to feel frighteningly real. Signs announcing the event appeared in shop windows in Monmouth, our nearest sizeable town. There were notices in the parish newsletter and the Grosmont Garden Club bulletin. Alan put an ad in the weekly *Beacon*. Shirley Jones started organizing the teas, Sheila Jones (no relation—Joneses are abundant in Wales) the plant stand. We decided to spend a couple of extra days at Towerhill Cottage for last-minute polishing, contemplation of weather reports, and unhappy discussions of just which of our special garden attractions would be past their prime. Among the latter, sadly, were the peonies, the glorious white *Clematis montana* covering the south end of the pergola, the *Ceanothus* 'Concha' on the south wall, and most of the kolkwitzia. But coming on fast were all sorts of roses (especially the 'Albéric Barbier'), some splendid cistuses, and enormous billows of 'Johnson's Blue' geraniums. Nothing fancy, but spectacular.

The catering operation swung into action in an orderly fashion. Tables and chairs, and a boiler for making tea, arrived from the village hall in a trailer pulled by Alan's tractor to be stacked in the garage (swept out for the occasion). Barbara Mitchley ordered cakes and got promises of others. Plant donations began accumulating at Sheila Jones's house in the village. Meanwhile, in the gardens of Towerhill Cottage, Carol finished up the bay hedge while I spent a morning edging beds with grass clippers and string-trimming anything that looked vulnerable. I had Marcus rake the lawn and mow it a second time. Theoretically, everything was under control; actually, I only had to turn around to see something else, usually major, that needed doing. The siding on the barn, for example, was warping badly: it really ought to be nailed down and given a fresh coat of stain. The raspberries unexpectedly started to ripen, to the delight of the blackbirds and to my horror: a netting cage was urgently called for. Dropping everything else, I built one.

Apart from a garden that doesn't measure up—and most people are too polite to complain out loud—nothing spoils a GARDEN OPEN day like rain. A few diehards will show up under umbrellas, but nobody else. At ten o'clock on the morning of June 15, just as the tea crew finished putting out chairs and tables and Sheila Jones was unloading trailerfuls of plants into the shelter of the woodshed, it started raining. Utter depression on our part. But this being Wales, of course, we should not have despaired. Within minutes the sun came out, dodging behind clouds for the rest of the day just the way the forecast had said it would.

Two o'clock was opening time. Would anybody come? Sure enough, at ten minutes before the hour a carful of women from Grosmont drove up the lane and parked in the meadow. More cars followed. I noticed a few weeds at the back of the new bed and nervously crawled under the lilacs to pull them out. When I stood up again, I was surprised to see that the place had suddenly become well populated. Visitors were wandering through the gardens peering and pointing, clustering around the plant stand buying everything from Japanese anemones (50p) to a potted *Salix daphnoides* (£3) and happily scoffing lemon cake and tea from the tables set out under the big walnut tree. There seemed to be a lot of children, too, chasing dogs and tossing balls back and forth.

So it went all afternoon—no rain, lots of visitors. By six o'clock, closing time, great inroads had been made upon the cakes and tea and the plant stand was decimated. Carol had been reduced to digging up abandoned clumps of 'Johnson's Blue' to supply the demand. I had heard no disparaging comments about the garden, in spite of the infantile state of the new bed (give it a couple more months and it should look fine), and nobody appeared to have tripped over an uneven flagstone or been lacerated by a rose. All of the bis-cuit tins supplied to hold money—for the teas, for the plants, for admission—were overflowing.

The takings, when they were added up later, came to no less than £400, which counts as a serious success. I'm still not wholly convinced that the teas didn't have more to do with it than the garden. But the village hall fundraisers were delighted. They'd like to have a GARDEN OPEN day again next year, and I suspect we'll go along. Who needs the Yellow Book, anyway?

II

Adventures in the

Vegetable Kingdom

THE GREAT WATER LILY

❧

*It has always been our endeavour to commence
a New Year in this Magazine with some emi-
nently rare or beautiful plant; but never had
we the good fortune on any occasion to devote
a Number to a production of such pre-eminent
beauty, rarity, and we may add celebrity, as
that now presented to our Subscribers. . . .
Seldom has any plant excited such attention in
the botanical world . . .*

The new year was 1846, and with these words the distinguished editor of *Curtis's Botanical Magazine* (and
director of Kew), Sir William Hooker, began a fresh volume. His enthusiasm was understandable, if uncharacteris-
tic. For the plant in question was indeed a marvel—the
biggest water lily anybody had ever laid eyes on, a spectacular monster described by one of the few Europeans to
see it blooming in its native habitat as "a vegetable wonder!" No more than a rumor for years, though a well-pub-
licized one, the plant was now at last alive and growing in
a warm pool at Kew, far from its South American home,
and proudly bearing the name of the Queen herself—
Victoria regia.

It was, as E. B. White's Charlotte might have said, some water lily. Boasting leaves up to six feet in diameter turned up at the edges to show their brilliant crimson undersides, it bore flowers as much as fifteen inches across that gave off an extraordinary rich pineapple scent. Of course, Sir William admitted, the plants growing at Kew hadn't actually flowered yet ("Many are the disappointments and delays of Science!"), but there was reason for hope, and dried specimens were available to substantiate—at least in part—the accounts of gob-smacked travelers.

Victoria had been a long time arriving in England. In fact, it had been a long time emerging from the stagnant backwaters of the Amazon basin where the German botanist Thaddäus Haenke, journeying through the region on a mission for the Spanish government, apparently first spotted it about 1801. He had reportedly fallen on his knees "in a transport of admiration" (a good trick, considering that he was traveling in a dugout canoe at the time). But if Haenke gathered specimens, they never reached Europe; all of his huge botanical collections vanished after his death in Bolivia in 1817.

Word, however, must have gotten round. About twenty years later, Aimé Bonpland, a French botanist, explorer, and colleague of the famous Alexander von Humboldt, discovered the *Victoria* growing in a river in the Argentinian province of Corrientes, near the Paraguayan border. He saw "this superb plant" at a distance, and (as Hooker put it) "well nigh precipitated himself off the raft into the river in his desire to secure specimens." Whether he got them or not is unclear; what is clear is that it was not until 1828 that another Frenchman, Aleide D'Orbigny, managed to send a collection of leaves, flowers, and seeds—some dried and some pickled in spirits—to the Museum of Natural History in Paris. Like Bonpland, D'Orbigny found his water lilies in Corrientes, and upon seeing them was "struck with profound emotion."

Unfortunately for D'Orbigny and the *gloire* of France, nobody in Paris got around to writing up and publishing his find. The specimens moldered away unremarked, to the point where nothing remained but a single gigantic leaf, "of immense dimensions and somewhat injured," Hooker reported, "which had been folded for insertion into the Herbarium." At this point, the French having blown it, the British stepped in.

Robert Schomburgk was, despite his name, at least an honorary Englishman. (He would eventually be knighted and serve as a British diplomat.) While still in his twenties, he left his native Germany to follow his interest in geography and natural history in the Caribbean and South America, choosing British territories to explore (there were plenty) and developing such a reputation that in 1831 the Royal Geographic Society commissioned him to make a survey of British Guiana. It was in the course of this investigation that, proceeding up the River Berbice "while contending with the difficulties that nature interposed in different forms," Schomburgk found a bay full of giant water lilies. "All calamities were forgotten; I was a botanist, and felt myself rewarded!" Unlike his predecessors he succeeded not only in collecting a variety of specimens—leaves, flowers, and fruit—but in getting them back to London. They were, it must be said, in a rather mangled and smelly state, yet not too far gone to be formally described by the botanist John Lindley, who published news of the discovery and firmly identified it as a new genus. This gave him the right to name it (much to French discomfiture), and he naturally chose to celebrate the newly crowned young queen.

Now the challenge was explicit: who would be the first in Britain—and it simply had to be Britain—to grow a live *Victoria* and watch it bloom? In 1845, the traveler Thomas Bridges, out shooting one afternoon in the interior of Bolivia, came upon a small pond filled with water lilies and alligators. Caution prevailed; he recruited some local men and a canoe before attempting to collect specimens of flowers, leaves, and seeds. Even so, it was a tricky business; the "tottering little bark" had room for only two of the huge leaves per trip, and when enough had been collected, he had to convince his doubtful helpers to haul the obviously useless load on carrying poles back to their village.

Bridges dried the leaves, preserved the flowers in spirits, and packed the seeds in wet clay, which was then thought to be the best way to keep them alive during the journey to England. En route, predictably, most of them went bad. But out of the twenty-two that Kew eagerly bought from him on arrival, two did germinate, calling forth Sir William's New Year effusion. The great water lily was alive and growing. The question was whether or not it would ever bloom before dying.

As the years passed, prospects became dimmer. The plants remained alive at Kew, but showed no signs of blooming. At this point, in the summer of 1849, a great gardener took over. Joseph Paxton—later Sir Joseph, and the genius behind the Crystal Palace—had been superintendent of the Duke of Devonshire's magnificent gardens at Chatsworth for many years. If anyone knew how to make a *Victoria* flower, it was Paxton; this was a man who had produced bananas in England for the ducal table. Chatsworth's famous "Great Stove"—a magnificent glass conservatory, the world's largest—had been built under his auspices. After constructing a special heated tank twelve feet square and three feet deep inside the conservatory, with a small water-wheel to keep the water moving gently, Paxton prevailed on Hooker to let him have one of the precious plants. He personally whisked it off to Chatsworth by fast train early one morning.

The duke was away at Lismore in Ireland as the drama began, but Paxton kept him posted. Planted in the new tank, the *Victoria* was tiny. Of its five leaves, the largest was less than six inches across. But it was clearly happier than at Kew, because within a month that leaf measured three and a half *feet* and was still growing. In another month it had hit four and a half feet, and the tank was getting distinctly crowded. Then, on the second of November, Paxton sent a triumphant message to Ireland: "Victoria has shown flower!! An enormous bud like a poppy head made its appearance yesterday. It looks like a large peach placed in a cup. No words can describe the grandeur and beauty of the plant."

And with that the water lily craze really took off. The duke hurried back from Ireland to witness the short-lived bloom—the first bud opened on the ninth of November, at night, and within thirty-six hours had decayed and sunk. Hooker came north, speeded by Paxton's assurance that "The sight is worth a journey of a thousand miles." Paxton presented Queen Victoria with a leaf and a new flower bud. Dozens of curiosity-seekers, titled and otherwise, turned up to gape, especially at the gigantic leaves, which were supposed to be able to support the weight of a human. In high spirits, the duke and Paxton dressed Paxton's seven-year-old daughter Annie as a fairy and stood her on one of the huge green saucers, inspiring the journalist Douglas Jerrold to a burst of Victorian sentimentality:

On unbent leaf in fairy guise,
Reflected in the water,
Beloved, admired by hearts and eyes,
Stands Annie, Paxton's daughter.

Accept a wish, my little maid,
Begotten at the minute,
That scenes so bright may never fade—
You still the fairy in it.

That all your life nor care nor grief
May load the wingéd hours
With weight to bend a lily's leaf,
But all around be flowers.

The image was unforgettable, so much so that perching a child on a *Victoria* leaf became a photographic cliché.

It suddenly seemed as though flowers were indeed "all around." Designers with an eye to the main chance quickly cobbled up lily motif fireplaces, chandeliers, and gas jet holders (Queen Victoria herself bought a bronze three-light gas bracket decorated with lilies). One art historian notes that "whole beds of water-lilies floated on Victorian floors, with the blue of the sky reflected enchantingly between the interstices of the lily-pads." Vases, pitchers, cups and saucers, even an entire lily-shaped baby's cradle made of papier-mâché (the "Victoria Regia Cot") answered public demand. Leaves and blossoms appeared on fabrics and wallpapers in such profusion as to suggest that the twining stems, if not the roots, of Art Nouveau lay here.

In the meantime, as if enjoying all the attention, the Chatsworth *Victoria* thrived, producing in the course of a year no less than 140 leaves, 112 flower buds, and many "fine plump seeds." To cultivate the new marvel properly, Paxton moved it from the Great Stove into a spacious new water-lily house, and before long Kew had a water-lily house too.

As it turned out, the lily was not all that hard to grow, provided the conditions were right. In America, spectacular *Victorias* could soon be found in water gardens from New Jersey south, even more vigorous for being cultivated outdoors. A championship specimen raised in St. Louis in 1896 reportedly produced a leaf capable of carrying a weight of 250 pounds. Botanists found other varieties in South America, and at Longwood Gardens in Pennsylvania, plant breeders developed V. 'Longwood Hybrid'.

These days you can still see V. *regia* (now distinguished from others of the genus by the name V. *amazonica*) blooming in a lily house at Chatsworth. The Great Stove, regrettably, is gone, dynamited by the ninth duke in 1919 in a fit of frustration at the number of precious plants lost in World War I fuel shortages. At Kew, *Victoria* has been at home since 1987 in the new Princess of Wales Conservatory.

Yet today the fashion for enormous water lilies with leaves that can support little girls seems to be fading, at least in Britain. Up until seven or eight years ago, in case you wanted something to startle the frogs in your pond, you could still buy a nursery-grown V. *amazonica*. Since then, according to that definitive manual *The Plant Finder*, they are no longer available. Perhaps it's just as well. Far from Victoria's fogbound kingdom, the famous Brazilian landscape architect Roberto Burle Marx has found more appropriate ways to use them in gardens, with great elegance and nothing of the freak show. I suspect that even Paxton might—after thinking about it—be prepared to step aside.

INVADERS

❧

I'm ashamed to say that I once raised a fine stand of Japanese knotweed in my garden in New England. I didn't know I was doing anything wrong; in fact, I was blissfully unaware until just the other day that it was Japanese knotweed at all. We called it bamboo. It certainly resembled bamboo, or some mutant New England version of bamboo—great fleshy jointed stalks, lavishly leaved, that shot up out of the earth each spring as if it couldn't wait to test the sunshine. In August came sprays of tiny white flowers that attracted bees while putting off the rest of us with a sickening sweet smell.

Perhaps I should have been suspicious. It did occur to me that the climate was entirely unsuited to bamboo, and there was something unnaturally aggressive about this stuff. Growing next to the front porch it was inoffensive enough, contending but generally losing in a battle for space with lilacs. But out by the barn, where I had decided to replace it with some mountain laurel brought down from Tom Ball Mountain, the "bamboo" refused to give up and go away. I chopped it down, dug out the roots, mowed shoots that poked up out of the lawn—and still it reappeared, with a sort of hurt "Did you miss me?" look. Eventually, by literally sifting the soil for fragments of root, I got rid of it. This took years.

It may be that where plants are concerned, I'm altogether too easygoing. If it's plausible—i.e., neither ugly, poisonous, nor covered in spikes—I'm inclined to leave it alone to get on with its duties in the Great Chain of Being. Thus moss and weeds in the lawn don't trouble me (from a distance they're all green), and I have a positive liking for ivy (in its place). Our garden here still features a large bulge of *Rhododendron ponticum* that I haven't had the heart to kill off in toto, not because we like to look at its glaring mauve blossoms, but simply because removing it would mean planting half a dozen square yards with something else that would doubtlessly require more care. It will go, sooner or later; according to some authorities it should be sooner, because ponticum is becoming a public nuisance in many wilderness and moorland regions of Britain.

Having traveled through bleak miles of it while touring the Scottish Highlands, I already had plenty of doubts about *R. ponticum*, but I've only recently become aware that there is a substantial contingent of introduced plants regarded as seriously bad news. That knotweed, for example. So far, I have not been troubled by it at Towerhill Cottage, but a hair-raising story in the *Times* the other day suggests that non-chalance is definitely not in order. When *Fallopia japonica* (better known to most gardeners as *Polygonum cuspidatum*) was brought to England from the Far East as an ornamental 150 years or so ago, it was thought to be infertile, because it arrived as a single female clone. Its habit of suckering and growing from tiny fragments of root, however, meant that reproduction was no problem, and now it has begun to crossbreed with such near relations as giant knotweed (*F. sachalinensis*) and Russian or mile-a-minute vine (*F. baldschuanica*). According to University of Leicester botanist John Bailey, some of the offspring of these matings—and even more unpredictable varieties produced by "back-breeding" between hybrids—could be tougher and more aggressive than the originals. (If you have ever owned, or been owned by, a Russian vine, you'll understand Bailey's concern.) Another problem is that the plethora of hybrids makes it improbable that a single natural pest capable of controlling knotweed will ever be found. While the helpful bug is crawling around looking for the knotweed, the hybrid may be racing up a tree.

The biggest news in the plant kingdom around here recently was doubtlessly the announcement that bracken spores can cause cancer. Bracken—that lovely big fern which now covers 2.5 million acres of the country (an area roughly the size of Yorkshire), including a good part of our wood—is spreading at a rate of up to three percent a year in some places in spite of struggles to control it. Sheep won't eat it. In the old days, farmers cut it regularly to use for animal bedding and thatch, and three cuttings a year are likely to tame it. But in recent times, there's not much call for bracken, apart from some tentative attempts to compost it and sell it as a peat substitute. The most obvious answer is a nontoxic herbicide called Asulox which, naturally, costs money. Until 1994, government grants were available to pay farmers to use it, but no longer in most places. So bracken spreads by great clouds of spores. From late August to early October, wear a face mask for a stroll through it, and any time of the year keep an eye out for ticks. Remember Lyme disease?

Nobody can be blamed for introducing bracken; it's been puffing spores into British air for millennia. Giant hogweed (*Heracleum mantegazzianum*) and Himalayan balsam (*Impatiens glandulifera*), on the other hand, were deliberately escorted through customs by gardeners and seedsmen early in the nineteenth century. For some years they behaved themselves in domestic circumstances, but balsam, in particular, seems to have harbored escapist tendencies. Equipped with an ability to fire its seeds more than thirty feet, it was soon populating river banks and damp places as far north as Scotland, and in the process swamping less vigorous native species. Travelers who have seen balsam in its Himalayan homeland say it is happier in England, where it can grow ten feet tall. I'm pleased to hear this, if only because I wouldn't want to imagine it being any bigger.

Giant hogweed has been causing a great fuss in England, first positive and then decidedly negative, for a century and a half. As Richard Mabey points out in *Flora Britannica*, the great garden writer John Claudius Loudon had nothing but praise for it ("magnificent umbelliferous plant . . . extremely interesting for the rapidity of its growth . . ."), while William Robinson found it "very suitable . . . for any place where bold foliage may be desired." Robinson, however, had an inkling of trouble ahead, observing that "when established they often sow themselves . . . it is important not to allow them to become giant weeds." And that, of course, is exactly what happened.

Clambering over the garden wall with some ease (each plant produces up to five thousand seeds), giant hogweed is now found virtually everywhere in Britain, often in huge, exclusive colonies. So far we have been spared it around Skenfrith, although it has turned up along the River Usk, twenty miles away. Some people, it is said, still grow it in their gardens, presumably for the sculptural effect; it looks like a fifteen-foot-tall cow parsnip (to which it is related). If you can stand its appearance, then you may also be able to put up with its unattractive habit of raising painful welts or burns on the skin of anybody foolish enough to touch it.

From such examples as these, it may seem obvious that carelessly introduced plants are a menace to the natural environment, bringing about the death of prized natives and leading to the botanical equivalent of suburban malls. Certainly that is the thesis projected by a fascinating little book called *Invasive Plants: Weeds of the Global Garden*, published recently by the Brooklyn Botanic Garden. From my point of view, the title is a bit deceptive, since the book deals only with plants troubling the United States, but what an array of potential crises and sleep-disturbers are here! I had no idea that I should be worrying about foxgloves (stretches of our wood are spiky with them) or buddleia or baby's breath or hawthorn (*Crataegus monogyna*), the last being your basic hedging plant in the Welsh Marches. In fact, of course, as a kindly botanist tells me, there's no need to get excited about the foxgloves and the hawthorn—they may be exotic imports in the United States, but they're innocent natives here. The scary stuff happens when a tough and adaptable plant finds itself—usually through man's agency—in a wholly new environment, becomes aggressive, and may very well do a lot of damage.

Whether this happens, however, generally depends as much on the vulnerability of the new ecosystem as it does on the character of the invader itself. I'm comforted by the fact that ours seems quite accommodating, possibly because it's anything but virginal. Man has been meddling with nature around here for more thousands of years than anybody can put a finger on, with the result that the whole place is, you might say, streetwise. In any case, there's an argument to be made for not getting excited. Mabey quotes research by the Botanical Society of the British Isles which suggests that few native species are at risk from invaders. He is himself "an unrepentant fan of opportunistic immigrants," which "act as buffers against climate change" and fill "man-made holes in our floral fabric." Personally, the only plant that really bugs me around Towerhill Cottage is the ubiquitous rosebay willow herb (*Epilobium angustifolium*), which has been spreading madly to the point that you can hardly pick blackberries in the fall without first disentangling them from the willow herb's fluffy seedheads, like milkweed floss. Rosebay willow herb is, so far as anyone knows, a native.

Before we leave the subject of invaders, there's one category that seems so far to have escaped mention. Last spring, on the tombstone page of our local paper, an announcement emanating from the Biotechnology Unit of the Department of the Environment advised us that a Belgian company called Plant Genetic Systems, N. V. had been granted permission to "release into the environment . . . genetically modified crop plants" at Great Crumbland Farm, Llanishen, Monmouth, namely oilseed rape plants genetically modified "to express male sterility or restored fertility." I can't pretend to know exactly what this means, or just how much of a good thing it is, but I'd rather that the Japanese knotweed didn't hear about it.

THE PERIPATETIC PEONY

❧

The big red peonies are collapsing. They've had their
day in the sun, or rather rain. A week of intermittent
heavy showers has left shattered heaps of petals sticking
wetly to the stone wall at the edge of the perennial bed, and
only a few of the massive blooms are still able to hold their
heads up. In a few days we must go round with the clippers
and finish the job. Peonies, as the expression goes, are generous. It may just be that they are overgenerous, considering
the spectacular and wholly impractical size of their blossoms.
They actually seem to be trying to please us, rather than the
bees. Because once those chunky buds have broken, a good
cloudburst is all it takes to bring on floral disaster.

No peony (no double peony anyway) is completely
immune to this dire scenario, but I am talking here about
the most common kind of *Paeonia officinalis*, the sort you
find growing everywhere in old cottage gardens in England.
In America, it is the familiar crimson "Memorial Day
peony," often appearing less luridly as pink. When we
arrived at Towerhill Cottage, there was a healthy clump
among the weeds; we have since split it up and replanted it
in various places, with no apparent diminution in its vigor,
although it took a year or two to start flowering again in a
new spot. In fact, I question whether you can kill the
thing—six or eight leftover roots abandoned in a bucket

even started to grow without soil before I put them out of their misery.

There is, of course, a lot more to peonies than these big red ones, pleasant and appropriate as they are. Even as the scarlet monsters are disintegrating, I'm waiting to see what will happen to another more precious specimen I've got growing in our garden. At the moment it has two buds— only one of them of a size likely to bloom—and instead of the lush coarse foliage of *officinalis*, a rather delicate collec-tion of stalks and very deeply cut leaves. This is a peony with a history. I planted it last October in the latest chapter of its extraordinary life.

My acquaintance with this particular peony began twenty-five years ago, when I bought a house in Western Massa-chusetts from a New York attorney named Frank Adams. Adams (or his wife—I was never quite sure) was a good gardener, judging from the plantings he turned over to us along with the keys to the house. Some of them (like a twisted and clearly aged quince) had been there a long time, but others had been more recently placed with an eye to effect and horticultural suitability. The peony was growing at the front of a small bed above a drystone retaining wall in a spot that was obviously well drained and enriched with manure.

One autumn day not long after we moved in, Adams came by to take away the peony. He had, I admit, warned me; that was a very special plant. Many years before, he explained, one of his wife's forebears had brought it over from England and installed it in the family garden near Boston. It flourished there, much admired. But as time passes, gardens—and gardeners—change. When in the 1950s Adams bought the house in the Berkshires, he made a point of rescuing the peony and bringing it west. Now he was moving again, down into Connecticut, and felt that he should take the peony along with him. It was, after all, a rare and extremely beautiful variety and wonderfully fragrant.

By this time, I had seen the peony in bloom and fully agreed with Adams's opinion of it. I was distressed to think of losing it. Being a nice man, Adams agreed to leave a few bits behind. I carefully dug them up and replanted them, at precisely the right depth, at several spots in the now-empty bed. In the spring spindly green shoots emerged, gradually bulked up, and before long the display was glorious as ever. For the next fifteen years, the peony went from strength to splendid strength.

In 1986 I moved to England. For various reasons, I had no opportunity to bring the peony. I often thought of it, though, and occasionally contemplated trying to identify it, so as to buy anther of the same kind here. At the Chelsea Flower Show one year, I went so far as to hunt diligently through a huge display of blooms in search of a variety like it. No luck; it was plainly too rare and unusual. My only hope, I figured, was somehow to get a piece of rootstock from the bed in the Berkshires and bring it back with me to England.

Finally, last fall I got the chance I'd been waiting for. On a sunny Sunday, visiting Alford for the first time in ten years, I dug up a good-sized piece of root with four or five eyes on it, convinced my brother-in-law to shake it in a bag with some powdered sulphur to sterilize it, wrapped it in a couple of layers of plastic, and sank it deep in my suitcase, between the socks and the undershorts.

In principle, smuggling plants is a lousy idea. I'll readily grant you that, even in the abstract. Eleanor Perényi describes how she managed to smuggle a couple of pounds of French *jaune d'hollande* seed potatoes into the United

States by mailing them to herself in a shoebox marked "shoes" and apparently got away with it. But after her account was reprinted in a magazine, so I'm told, the law descended. Ms. Perényi found her vegetable garden placed under strict quarantine for two years. I suppose the same thing might—unfairly—happen to my peony.

Yet as I pushed my trolley unchallenged through customs at Heathrow with the peony root stashed among the socks, I felt nothing but satisfaction. My enterprise was restoring an unusual plant to its native place and, moreover, adding to its improbable story. Think of it! Britain to Boston to the Berkshires to Britain! If I got it to grow, the circle would be closed. I would have both a rare peony and a sentimental reminder of New England.

Moreover, once the peony bloomed I'd be able to identify it. Some book, some expert would be able to tell me. It would be exciting to know just how rare it was. I could remember a lot about it—its wonderful scent, its brilliant coloring, the size and abundance of its blossoms. But identification is a tricky business, and even an expert was likely to insist on seeing the real thing.

Well, I was wrong. A few weeks ago, long before the peony bloomed (if indeed it ever does), we spotted a garden in the Yellow Book that sounded, in the circumstances, well worth going to visit. Green Cottage, in Lydney, advertised itself as having "many herbaceous paeonies, including the National Reference Collection of pre- and early post-1900 cultivars." I had decided that peonies were something worth knowing more about. You can only learn so much from books, although I had already learned that if you count the number of buds on your peony and come out with an odd number, someone is going to die. A somewhat more dependable source advised that the first peony to appear in

England came from the Eastern Mediterranean, possibly Crete, about 1548 and was a red single. (The classic double crimson *P. officinalis* turned up in Antwerp as a chance mutation soon after.) John Gerard, the sixteenth-century plantsman who was a good gardener but a plagiarist, planted peony seeds surreptitiously so that he could claim (unsuccessfully, I gather) to have discovered a new English wildflower.

Although it had been an early spring, the peonies at Green Cottage (except for a few *officinalis*) were not yet in bloom the day we arrived. One large bed contained the National Reference Collection of Pre- and Early Post-1900 peonies, the plants growing in rows like so many vegetables, with stakes and stretched wires to keep them from falling over. Their names sounded like a guest list from Proust: 'Duchesse de Nemours', 'Général MacMahon', 'Félix Crousse', 'Madame Calot', 'Monsieur Martin Cahazac', 'Inspecteur Lavergne'. But there was no way even to guess what they would look like when the buds opened. If I was going to find my peony here, I'd have to come back a few weeks later.

As we were leaving we encountered Mrs. Baber, who was tending a small collection of plants for sale in her garage. No peonies for sale were in evidence, but when she noticed us eyeing some potted specimens beneath a wire netting nearby, she asked if we had come a long way and wanted peonies. We assured her that we were simply browsing (buying unneeded plants is all too easy) and got talking about her great love and how she sometimes imports rare specimens from a breeder in Washington State. This discussion led naturally to my telling her about my precious peony and its adventures.

What did it look like? she asked. I described what I remembered of its huge white blossoms, the flecks of scarlet, the amazing perfume, its obvious rarity. Mrs. Baber smiled. Was it a true bright "ice" white, not cream? Were the flecks of red at random, sometimes deep among the petals? I agreed that they were. "'Festiva Maxima'!" she said firmly. "No doubt about it. It can't be anything else."

So much for rarity. Far from being unusual, Mrs. Baber explained, 'Festiva Maxima' is one of the most common peony cultivars and has been since it was bred in France in 1851. Whole fields of it are grown in the Channel Islands for cutting and export to florists' shops. Dozens of nurseries carry them in this country; checking an American catalogue, I see 'Festiva' described as "The old reliable white . . . One of the most generally planted Peonies in cultivation."

I'm not too unhappy about this. Even Mrs. Baber, whose taste in peonies is about as refined as you can get, admits that 'Festiva Maxima' is a wonderful plant, scarcely bettered, and well worth growing even if the whole neighborhood is growing the same thing. I trust it will thrive at Towerhill Cottage. In the meantime, I have developed a strong interest in peonies and intend to try some more. They needn't be rare, by the way.

ORPHAN SEEDS

※

Making fun of Oscar Wilde in *Patience*, Gilbert and Sullivan brought the house down with a song about their hero Bunthorne's slightly kinky lust "for a bashful young potato, or a not-too-French French bean." A few weeks ago, reality took a step in the same direction. The Prince of Wales, who is famously fond of gardening (he talks to his plants), made the front page of the *Times* with a public appeal for Britons to "Adopt a Veg." It was no joke.

The problem of orphaned vegetables began, as so many problems the British have to contend with these days do, with the slow but apparently inexorable move toward European political union. While a single super-state does not yet exist in any final way, for thirty or forty years various international commissions and organizations have been devising regulations and issuing directives covering almost every field of human activity and giving them the status of law. Inevitably, horticulture felt the lash.

Back in the 1960s, when the European Community bureaucrats in Brussels first took up the subject of vegetable varieties, it was admittedly bogged in confusion—too many names, many of them ambiguous or duplicative; undependable cultivars; general uncertainty about just what was likely to come up when you planted a seed. Dealers were selling the same seeds under entirely different names (at one point you could buy a common variety of lettuce under forty names) or different seeds under the same name. Systematizing things made a lot of sense.

Too much sense, as it turned out. After a few years of consulting and counting, the agricultural commissioners came up with a gilt-edged list of varieties whose seeds could be sold freely. Each country had its own National List, and these were then amalgamated into a master Common Catalogue that in its latest (sixteenth) edition runs to nearly five hundred pages. Most of the familiar varieties are there, from 'Tendergreen' bush beans to 'Iceberg' lettuce, and also some unfamiliar ones—how about 'Baby Fun' watermelon? or 'Sälzmunder Edelperle' peas? But not everything. Indeed, that is the catch. Because if a seed is not listed, the rules say that it can't be sold legally. It is, literally, a botanical outcast.

What's important is that getting a particular vegetable variety cleared for sale—that is, introduced into the National List—is a serious undertaking. These days a seedsman must pay a hefty initial fee (up to £1,800 or $2,880) and then £150 ($240) a year to maintain the listing. This is meant to cover costs, including two years of field trials by the Ministry of Agriculture to establish that the variety is actually different and that it is uniform in size, yield, appearance, and flavor. The consequences of this practice, as even the most desk-bound Brussels bureaucrat might have predicted, have been dire.

To be worth registering, a vegetable variety must sell well enough to pay its way, and you don't need higher math to see that you have to flog a great many packets of 'Miss Warden's Perpetual' kale seed to pay off the basic nut, much less clear a profit. The simplest solution, and one which most seed companies are forced to adopt whether they want to or not, is to give up offering the variety for sale. This process has been going on at a great rate.

Nobody knows the exact number of vegetable varieties extant—there are untold thousands—but only about three thousand are listed in the Common Catalogue and for sale in Britain. All the rest are by definition illegal and their seeds can't be sold. In many cases, however, these outcasts are desirable, especially to ordinary home gardeners. Large-scale commercial vegetable growers may well favor varieties of green beans or lettuces that produce their entire crop at one time—that saves picking time. They may prefer a kind of pea that never grows higher than four feet, six inches, so the picking machines can operate efficiently. And they may want a tough-skinned (possibly square) tomato that ripens slowly after being picked—it makes shipping a lot easier. The way the list works, the big growers get what they want.

As things have predictably turned out, the same can't always be said for the amateurs. Jeremy Cherfas, head of genetic resources at the Henry Doubleday Research Association (HDRA), notes that if, for example, a home gardener wants to grow peas taller than four feet, six inches, say the 150-year-old 'Champion of England' variety, the seed isn't available commercially. If he wants to experiment with a 'Blacktail Mountain' watermelon or a potato known as 'Bishop's Choirboys', tough luck; not on sale. If he prefers to pick his green beans repeatedly in small quantities over a long period, thus avoiding a glut, he may no longer be able to buy a variety tending to bear that way. In fact, the controls are so strict that a vast number of such old, rare, and uncommon varieties are in serious danger of vanishing entirely.

The dodges have proved to be complicated and not altogether satisfactory. In 1993, the big Ipswich seed merchants

Thompson and Morgan were hauled into court and prose-
cuted on four counts of selling unlisted seed bred for growing giant competition vegetables. The judge, as one report
put it, found them "guilty on all four vegetables," but gave
them a conditional discharge provided they stopped mar-
keting the seed. Thompson and Morgan's response, which
they seem to have gotten away with, involved labeling the
seed packets with a disclaimer saying "Available for test purposes only. Please report back to us on performance."

The principal way of making the seeds of unlisted varieties available, however, is to give them away. This is the
strategy of HDRA, a private foundation based in Ryton,
near Coventry, which has for years been devoting its energies to attacking and subverting the EC regulations.
Anyone can subscribe to their Heritage Seed Program and
be eligible to "borrow" seeds of some seven hundred old but
good unlisted varieties they keep in their seed library, sometimes (but not necessarily) returning fresh seed to the
library after harvest. The names alone are enough to convince me that this is a great idea: 'Daniel's Defiance' runner
bean, 'Bedford Market Rearguard' brussels sprout, 'Lazy
Housewife' climbing French bean (a green bean or snap
bean to Americans), 'Laird's Victory' turnip, 'Silsden Bomb'
cabbage, 'Tiger Tom' tomato. Until now, potatoes have not
been included (a seed potato is, after all, a potato and not a
seed), but HDRA is expanding the library to take them in.
Then any subscriber will have access to a 'Himalayan Red'
or a 'Ballydoon' to try in his or her garden—perfectly legally.

In the last few years, attempts have been made to restore
some sanity to the EC seed regulations. Proposals to ease
restrictions on varieties sold in very small quantities, however, have failed to pass, stymied by arguments over what "a
small quantity" is. (Draft directives quoted by Cherfas sug-

gested a two-kilogram annual limit, but did not distinguish between two kilos of lettuce seed—"Enough to plant the whole of southern England"—and two kilos of seed potatoes. "Daft and impossible," Cherfas fumes.) There is even an ominous rumor of new controls on seeds distributed free, forbidding gardeners from growing to produce more seed. Eating your 'Abraham Lincoln' tomatoes will be okay, but not if you collect the seeds for reuse or return to the library.

In the meantime, Prince Charles's "Adopt a Veg" appeal is intended to raise money for the HDRA move into potatoes and to help put the seed library as a whole on a more stable footing. For £12.50, a donor will be named official godparent to any one of the listed varieties stocked. For £250 he can befriend as many as six, in the process gaining the title of Veg Champion (and presumably a great opportunity to meet a bashful young potato).

Satisfying an allotment gardener's yearning for 'Christmas Purple Sprouting' broccoli like his grandmother used to grow might seem to be the point of all this, but as Jeremy Cherfas makes plain, it isn't. Preserving old varieties of vegetables is just another way of preserving genetic diversity, and that is desperately important. In the introduction to a handy guide called *The Veg Finder*, which lists all the commercially available vegetable varieties in the United Kingdom and tells where to buy seeds, Cherfas reports the sad case of the British potato. Only six varieties represent roughly two-thirds of the acreage planted to early potatoes. Nearly half of all main crop potatoes are another three varieties. These are the potatoes you can buy in the store. But they are also the ones by far easiest to find as seed potatoes. Of 150 varieties listed as available, only thirty-one can be found at more than five suppliers. Eighty-one of the 150 are only available from single suppliers.

Now while Wilja, Maris Bard, and Cara are all good potatoes (I've grown them myself), by reducing the number of generally available varieties to so few we are running the risk of a disaster on the order of the Irish Potato Famine. That, Cherfas points out, resulted from the fact that all the potatoes grown in Europe in the 1840s descended from just two Andean strains, both of which were susceptible to late blight. Late blight arrived from Mexico. Bang. Recently another strain of blight from Mexico has been reported abroad, the first for 150 years.

In *Green Thoughts*, Eleanor Perényi calls genetic diversity nature's first line of defense against pests, diseases, and adverse climatic conditions. She draws a vivid analogy between our narrowing pool of plant varieties and a royal family, having pursued a policy of intermarriage, being left with a bunch of hemophiliacs and congenital idiots. This may be overstating the case for the 'Lazy Housewife' bean, but possibly not.

MISTLETOE

❀

It would have been nice if the whole affair had been just slightly more Christmasy. There ought to have been Yule logs, deep snow, and a few escapees from Dickens at the very least. But what we had instead was piercing damp, sullen gray skies, half an inch of sticky red mud, and a lot of serious men carrying notebooks and wearing soft caps and Wellies. More Breughel than Boz. And, of course, an entire stockyard lot full of "wraps" (bundles) of holly and mistletoe, being drizzled on and waiting to go under the auctioneer's hammer at the Tenbury Wells Holly and Mistletoe Sale.

Mistletoe is a very odd, almost entirely useless plant. For at least nine-tenths of the year, nobody wants it, presumably including the trees it grows on as a parasite. But as Christmas approaches, mistletoe comes into its own. So one shouldn't necessarily be surprised that so much of it has fetched up here in Tenbury Wells in a yard belonging to Russell, Baldwin and Bright (usual business sheep, cattle, houses, and farms). Every florist in Britain will want at least a few sprigs to sell, and Tenbury Wells, the mistletoe capital, is the place where many wholesale dealers go to stock up.

I came to this auction—one of three or four that are held each year in late November and early December—to meet Stanley Yapp. Yapp is, you might say, the "Voice of Mistletoe." A stocky, amiable farmer living a few miles west of

Tenbury, he has become quite remarkably obsessed with mistletoe. He is an expert on its rich mythology and history and has even been known to compose poetry in praise of his favorite plant. When mistletoe goes on sale in Tenbury Wells, Yapp is sure to be there. "It's a social occasion"—but it is also clearly a time to find out just what is happening in the market.

So far as Yapp and his friends are concerned, the most threatening thing that's happening in the mistletoe market these days is the French invasion. Traditionally, English mistletoe is cut from English trees, but it is getting harder to find, and apple orchards in Brittany are full of it. French apple farmers, moreover, are apparently convinced that mistletoe harms their trees, and have no qualms about cutting it. Their only problem is selling it, because you don't *fêter Noël* with mistletoe. So the French mistletoe is packed into cabbage crates and shipped directly to English wholesalers, sometimes spending a month or two in cold store en route. It is not welcome at Tenbury Wells ("We don't want it here—and the Frenchies can keep their milk, too"). I saw only half a dozen crates, and its quality was plainly lower than that of the local variety, with fewer berries and hangdog foliage that may have been affected by a spell in deep freeze. Ironically, a French truckers' strike and a fire in the Channel Tunnel reduced the amount exported this year, but it still reportedly depressed the British market price. One Conservative member of Parliament went so far as to call for a boycott.

For at least seventy-five years, and probably much longer, English mistletoe collectors have been scavenging the old apple orchards of the Welsh Marches—Shropshire, Gloucestershire, especially Herefordshire and Worcestershire—and bringing their clumps and bundles of *Viscum album* to

Tenbury Wells for auction. Traditionally, Stanley Yapp ex-
plains, most of the collectors are gypsies, "traveling people"
who make their living picking fruit and vegetables in season.
For them, mistletoe—less a crop then a sort of free-for-the-
picking spin-off—is a nice little earner.

I had originally been referred to Yapp when I was trying
to find out something about propagating mistletoe. Out of
the flood of information Yapp provided, I was able to piece
together some essential facts, the main one being that
human beings *can* propagate mistletoe, but a bird—the mis-
sel thrush (*Turdus miscivorus*)—does the job much better.
Dining on a white berry, which is filled with a sticky paste-
like substance, he wipes his beak on a branch, leaving seeds
embedded in a crevice in the bark. The mistletoe then
sprouts, sending rootlets into the host tree and drawing
upon it for necessary mineral nutrients.

I have since learned that it is possible to "inoculate" a
tree by smearing a well-placed mistletoe berry on a branch,
although I haven't tried it; the garden writer Ursula Buchan
points out that the best time to do this is March or April,
when the seeds are ripe, but by then your Christmas sprig
will be well over the hill. According to Plantlife, a charity
devoted to saving wild plants and their habitats, "there is no
guaranteed method . . . some [people] are successful, but
many remain disappointed."

With the help of birds, however, a very wide range of
species is hospitable to mistletoe. The most common hosts
are old apple trees, small leaf limes (*Tilia cordata*), hawthorns,
poplars, false acacias (*Robinia pseudoacacia,* what Americans
call black locust), field maples (*Acer campestre*), crack wil-
lows (*Salix fragilis*), and ashes, while more exotic species from
cotoneasters to horse chestnuts occasionally stand in. Yet
even so, some species resist, most famously the oaks.

Mistletoe in an oak tree is a rarity, so much so that the association has accumulated its own heavy load of legend and myth. Just how much of this lore is authentically ancient and how much the result of latter-day antiquarianism may be open to question, but some authorities (Stanley Yapp is one) will tell you that mistletoe found growing in an oak was so sacred to the druids that it had to be cut with a golden knife, allowed to fall on a white cloth held by virgins, and taken away in a cart pulled by white bulls, which were subsequently sacrificed. Pliny, the Roman natural historian, reported this first. It makes a good story, and certainly mistletoe in an oak is hard to find. I thought I saw some the other day, but it turned out to be a clump of ivy.

According to Richard Mabey, mistletoe traditions are among northern Europe's last surviving fragments of plant magic. The practice of kissing under it is thus supposed to be a debased or soft-core echo of its original function as an aphrodisiac and the source of a fertility potion. It was regarded as a cure for epilepsy and measles, with an ability to reduce tumors and fend off witches. Farmers treated sheep and cattle with it. Yapp recalls how in the Tenbury neighborhood it was customary to take down the mistletoe after Twelfth Night, set it alight, and then run with the burning branch across the nearest field of growing grain, thereby assuring a good crop. Powerful stuff! Until recently—no more than thirty years ago—mistletoe could not even be used to decorate churches in some parishes, Mabey says, because of its pagan implications.

Nevertheless, just as Clement Moore and "The Night Before Christmas" probably has more to do with our modern notion of Santa Claus than any amount of ancient folklore, the association between mistletoe and Christmas appears to be of relatively modern origin. In those parts of

England and Wales where it commonly grew, local traditions usually connected it to New Year celebrations and the period running up to Candlemas (February 2). In the eighteenth century, a Rev. William Stukeley popularized druidism as a sort of primitive Christianity, creating a fad that spread through the country and incidentally tying mistletoe (and kissing) firmly to the holiday season. In naming his enormous treatise on primitive beliefs *The Golden Bough* (mistletoe turns golden after being hung up for a few months), Sir James Frazer simply complicated matters.

Still, if you are lucky enough to see a pale yellow-green cascade of mistletoe growing from the otherwise bare branches of an apple tree on an icy midwinter day, surrounded by a chirruping flock of birds feeding on the berries, it will be obvious why this plant came to be regarded with a certain uncomfortable respect. At a time when everything else was dead, it was alive and even flowering; normal plants rooted themselves in the earth, while it seemed to live on air. I'm delighted to note that our biggest apple tree at Towerhill Cottage is now host to a small spray (still berryless—it may need a partner) and that an old orchard down in the valley near Skenfrith has half a dozen splendid clusters that the gypsies have apparently not yet spotted.

Yet there are hints that in Britain as a whole mistletoe is scarcer than it used to be, even a few years ago. While prices at Tenbury Wells did not reflect this (only 50p to 75p—85¢ to $1.25 per pound average), serious shortages were reported in London last Christmas, and there was almost nothing left to collect in some hitherto fruitful areas. What remains is more and more found far above ground in tall trees. Attempts—doubtfully successful, as you might guess—have been made to harvest such high clumps by shotgun.

Together with the Botanical Society of the British Isles, Plantlife recently conducted a major survey of mistletoe, the first since 1970, on the plausible presumption that it may someday—if not already—be an endangered species. Calculations are not yet complete, but according to Jonathan Briggs, who is coordinating the data, it isn't quite time for panic stations. Dots on the sightings map in mistletoe's West Country heartland seem to be farther apart than they were twenty-five years ago, but more reports could still close some of the gaps. What the preliminary findings have done is to confirm distribution patterns and show that elderly full-size apple trees remain the favorite host, harboring nearly forty percent of all sightings.

This ancient alliance may represent the most serious threat to mistletoe's future. All through the rolling orchard-covered hills of the Marches, aged apples are being grubbed out and replaced with smaller bush-type trees less welcoming to mistletoe and more easily harmed by it. In the end, it may not be the gypsies lugging Christmas bundles to Tenbury Wells that spells oblivion for this botanical oddity in Britain, but the hybridizers, the efficiency experts, and the man who invented the mechanical apple picker.

THE LOST ORCHID

❦

In a couple of weeks, our orchids will be peeping up out of the grass in a corner of the orchard. Every year there are a few more, purple spikes four or five inches high that you must hunt for. They are early-purple orchids, what Shakespeare referred to as "long purples" in Ophelia's bouquet, and are relatively common. "Relatively," of course, is the operative word here, because no orchid growing in the wild is really common, in England or anywhere else. When we consider the more glamorous tropical orchids, moreover, true rarity is the word.

So far as I know, no British orchid has ever been found, named and described, and then lost again, vanishing into a limbo of speculation and legend from which it might or might not ever emerge. Among tropical orchids, however, this has happened more than once. For nearly fifty years, for example, a *Paphiopedilium* called *P. fairieanum* was lost. It had first turned up in a London sale room in 1855, was exhibited and admired at a Royal Horticultural Society show, but could not be propagated and, in spite of a £1,000 reward, could not be located in the wild again. A band of surveyors eventually came across it once more in Bhutan in 1904.

But the best case of a lost orchid, the really classic case that brackets the whole era of "orchidomania," is that of the spectacularly beautiful *Cattleya* known as *C. labiata vera—*

the last word (meaning "true") tacked on by frustrated botanists to distinguish it from the many near relatives found while it remained lost.

The "tulipomania" that swept Holland in the seventeenth century saw collectors bid up the price of rare bulbs to bankrupting levels. While it never reached quite that degree of hysteria, a similar craze agitated horticultural circles in nineteenth-century England. This time it involved orchids, and was stimulated in the first place by the accidental import, to a gardener living near London, of some pieces of root and stem that struck him as interesting.

In 1818, like most people at the time, William Cattley apparently knew little about tropical orchids, although examples had been trickling into the country at an increasing rate for close to a century, brought by explorers like Sir Joseph Banks. How to grow them was a mystery. With no knowledge of their original habitat, nurserymen tended to plunge them into tanbark for the sake of warmth and keep them as damp and airless as possible. Being epiphytes, which live an airy, semiparasitical life high off the ground on the trunks or branches of trees, most of them predictably faltered and died under this treatment. England, as Kew's Sir Joseph Hooker was to observe ruefully a few years later, was "the grave of tropical orchids."

Cattley, however, had better luck with his specimen (which, as was much later learned, is one of the easier orchids to cultivate). It had turned up as packing material in a box of lichens sent to him from Rio by a naturalist named Swainson. In the autumn of 1818, Cattley managed to bring it into flower. It was, he exclaimed, "The most splendid, perhaps, of all Orchidaceous plants." The botanist John Lindley, agreeing, published a description and named it in Cattley's honor: *Cattleya labiata*, for its pronounced lip.

As collectors in the field got busy searching for more *C. labiata*, its reputation spread. The few available divisions from Cattley's original plant gradually died off until there were none left. Rare examples mysteriously turned up from time to time at auction, bringing higher and higher prices— in 1870 £31 (the equivalent in dollars today of $2,300), in 1880 39 guineas ($2,800). Meanwhile, other kinds of tropical orchids arrived—from South America, Southeast Asia and India, Africa, Australia—many of them exquisite. Rich connoisseurs eagerly followed the example of the Duke of Devonshire and his unparalleled collection at Chatsworth, vying with each other for the finest and most unusual plants. Dealers hastened to supply them. Propagation being difficult if not impossible, this meant sending orchid hunters out to likely locations and taking plants from the wild.

It is difficult to imagine the scale on which this was done. Vast areas were denuded, not only of orchids but of the trees that bore them, chopped down so that collectors could reach the plants. A single expedition to Colombia in search of *Odontoglossum crispum* felled four thousand trees to collect ten thousand orchids. In 1878, one London dealer announced the arrival of two consignments containing a total of two million plants. Entire orchid-rich areas of Central and South America have been without orchids since. There were a few voices of protest: "This is no longer collecting," said the director of the Botanical Garden of Zurich. "It is wanton robbery."

Amid the destruction, botanists did at least learn more about the orchid family. Where in 1823 only 134 species were known, in the year 1837 alone 300 new species were introduced. (In 1852, Lindley would estimate the total in existence to be about six thousand—and this was an underestimate.) But of the precious *C. labiata*, nothing. Swainson had not been specific about the place he found Cattley's plant, although it was assumed to have been somewhere near Rio. In 1836, a naturalist named George Gardner, working in the Organ Mountains fifteen miles inland from Rio, found what he thought was the right Cattleya, and collected it "with much difficulty and no little danger" from the edge of a precipice. Unfortunately, Gardner brought back only a few living plants (which were probably the wrong ones anyway), and by the time professional collectors got there, the site had been stripped for charcoal-burning and coffee plantations.

Orchid hunters found other Cattleyas—C. *mossiae*, C. *mendelii*, C. *trianaei*, C. *dowiana*, and more. Against the usual odds of tropical fevers, bandits, unfriendly locals, and lack of transport, they collected the plants and shipped them off to London and Paris, where the few that survived went to auction. But no *vera*, no *true* Cattleya. From time to time, one would come to light in the glasshouses of rich men like Lord Douglas-Home and Lord FitzWilliam; two appeared in the London Zoological Gardens in Regent's Park (the theory was that they had something to do with a shipment of South American monkeys); the Imperial Gardens in St. Petersburg flowered a few, but the director didn't know or wouldn't say where they had come from.

All this time, as auction prices for rare orchids soared, dealers continued to press their agents to locate the precious Cattleya. Competition between orchid hunters was already intense, sometimes brutal, frequently involving spies and sabotage. (A favorite trick: pay a dock worker to urinate on a shipment of packed plants, causing them to bolt en route and be worthless on arrival.) By the 1860s, thanks to Lindley's research on habitats and the horticultural skills of the Duke of Devonshire's great gardener

Joseph Paxton, growers learned ways of cultivating the higher-altitude cool-weather species, and a flood of Andean varieties entered the picture. But that Cattleya still beckoned. Frederick Sander, the principal orchid dealer, with huge storehouses in England and Belgium, instructed his men to scour the Rio area, follow Gardner's and Swainson's tracks, and hunt through every plausible part of Colombia and Venezuela. One persistent fellow spent five years exploring the entire coastline of Brazil, without luck.

The sort of excitement involved in the search emerges clearly from letters quoted by Arthur Swinson in his biography of Sander. For example, in December 1881, one of Sander's hunters, William Arnold, found a Cattleya in Venezuela that he thought might be C. *labiata vera*. "Keep your gob shut," Sander wrote to him. "1,000 plants would be worth £10,000 if they arrive and are genuine. A fortune! But silence . . . I am extremely excited about all this and the battle with White [a rival orchid hunter], although I wish he had yellow fever! I know you won't be outdone by him." In the event the long-suffering Arnold wasn't outdone; he managed to ship a thousand plants to Sander, whose delight was constrained only by the poor condition in which they arrived. "The whole world's mad on Cattleya at the moment," he wrote. "MOUTH SHUT!" Then the anticlimax: word came from the distinguished expert Professor Heinrich Gottlieb Reichenbach, to whom Sander had submitted sample for analysis, that the Cattleya wasn't *vera* after all, but a new variety.

Nevertheless, it was Sander who finally reintroduced the "true" Cattleya. Its native home was found to be the rainforests of Pernambuco, a thousand miles or so away from Rio. But if the place is indisputable, the circumstances of the plant's rediscovery are murky indeed, encrusted with tall stories and legend. One pleasant version has an orchid fancier spotting it in the corsage of a lady at an embassy ball in Paris and tracking it to its source. A marginally more plausible account has Sander seeing the plant in a naturalist's greenhouse in Paris, asking where it came from, and then sending one of his collectors to the spot (possibly the unfortunate Arnold, who later disappeared up the Orinoco). Whatever the truth of the matter, by the end of 1893 Sander had plenty of *Cattleya labiata vera* to sell and no incentive at all to give details about just where they had come from.

Almost overnight, the rare Cattleya became commonplace. Relatively simple to cultivate and decadently gorgeous, it quickly caught the fancy of elegant women in Paris and London. Readers of Proust will remember how in *Swann's Way* the Cattleya was not only the fascinating Odette's favorite flower; it had a private meaning for the lovers in the phrase "do a cattleya," referring to what ensued when Swann undertook to arrange her corsage.

Today C. *labiata* may be the best known of all tropical orchids, so much so that some writers betray a slight irritation in talking about it. "The only orchid with which the average layman is at all familiar," grumbles one, rapidly going on to speak of more interesting species. "Plentiful today—too much so, the cut flower growers say," complains another. Tell that to poor Arnold, sixty feet up a tree in Pernambuco.

NETTLES

⚜

"Long live the weeds," wrote the poet Gerard Manley Hopkins, whose romantic nature led him up more than one leafy blind alley. Possibly he had dandelions or corn poppies in mind, maybe—at a stretch—a thistle. But one thing's certain: he must have overlooked *Urtica dioica*, better known as the stinging nettle. Otherwise, the only appropriate response to his vegetable cheer is John McEnroe's famous refrain, "You can *not* be serious."

According to the books, stinging nettles are common in the United States, having been imported (presumably accidentally) by early settlers, but I can honestly say that I never ran across them in any memorable way until I moved to Britain. In the Berkshires, nettles weren't much of a menace. They meant so little, in fact, that when I spotted my first large patch bordering a path on the edge of our woods in Skenfrith, I wasn't sure what they were. I very quickly found out.

Carol is convinced that my remarkable susceptibility to nettle stings is due to the fact that I didn't grow up with them the way she did in Ireland. She's practically immune, whereas if I merely brush against a nettle leaf I can still feel the painful prickles twelve or fifteen hours later. Careless weeding without gloves can have major consequences, while any larger endeavors involving nettles require as much forethought as a sally into a bed of poison ivy. I have even succeeded in getting my forehead nettled, which you have to admit takes some doing. (I was crawling under a barbed wire fence with a fly rod at the time.)

According to *The Flora of Monmouthshire*, a fascinating compilation largely composed of records made by local amateurs with a taste for botany, the normal habitat for stinging nettles in our part of the country is "Roadsides, hedgerows, wood borders and waste places"—in other words, every place. They are "very common in all districts." This is nothing more than the truth. Nettles are unavoidable.

One problem seems to be that they have no competent antagonists. Most animals won't eat them, for obvious reasons (although my farmer neighbor claims that sheep will eat them after they're cut), and apart from the caterpillars of a few kinds of butterfly (the comma is one), insects don't pay much attention to them either. Normal plants, needing insect contact to pollinate them, might find this lack of interest awkward, but not nettles: they boast an ingenious self-pollinating system involving spring-loaded anthers that simply toss the pollen into the air, whereupon the wind carries it where nature intends it to go. It is said that on a calm morning, you can sometimes see nettle pollen puffing out like tiny fountains.

There was a time when mankind regarded nettles more positively than we (or at least I) are inclined to do today. Fibers from the lanky stems were twisted into rope and woven into cloth, especially in Northern Europe, until surprisingly recently; before World War I, the Germans were harvesting up to sixty thousand tons of nettles a year to make soldiers' uniforms. (If this sounds penitential, it isn't: boiling renders the nettle stingless.) Some American Indians did the same. In the early 1940s, as part of the war effort, county herb committees in England called for one hundred tons of nettles to be gathered. Mystified local collectors obliged, discovering only later that the leaves would be used for green camouflage dyes and chlorophyll extracts.

Such practical activities don't appear to have made much impact on the nettle population, nor did the ancient use of nettles for food. Nettle soup, which calls for the earliest tender tops of the plants to be plucked and boiled in stock or other liquid, has always had a following. In Ireland during the potato famine, starving peasants scoured the fields and ditches for nettles to eat, while in happier circumstances the Scots savored nettle pudding: nettle tops, leeks, onions, oats, and brussels sprouts, served with butter or gravy. (Sounds like you could leave out the nettles.) When the diarist Samuel Pepys stopped in to see his friend William Symons one cold winter day in 1661, Symons's wife thoughtfully served him a dish of freshly made "nettle porrige," which Sam—who fancied himself a connoisseur— thought "very good."

Books of plant lore are full of received wisdom about the medical virtues of nettles. The doctrine of plant "signatures"—which held that every plant had some human use, and that its shape, color, or other characteristic would tell you what that use was—suggested that nettles were just the thing for skin ailments, and probably wouldn't do rheumatism any harm. The treatment was flogging with a bunch of nettles. (There is a doubtful theory that the plants came to Britain in the first place with Roman soldiers who lashed themselves with nettles for warmth during the un-Italian weather.) Nettle seeds mixed with wine (how much wine?) were supposed to treat impotence, and nettle ale was taken to be a cure for jaundice. A gypsy prescription even employed nettles as a contraceptive. The man was supposed to line his socks with nettle leaves and wear them for 24 hours before engaging in sex. If this worked, it may have been for the wrong reasons.

On the whole, though, nettles have never had a very good press. "What could be more odious than nettles?" asked the Roman naturalist Pliny the Elder, hardly expecting an answer, and anybody who has suffered a good stinging would heartily agree. (I include here anyone unfortunate enough to have met up with what must be the world's nastiest nettle, *Urtica urentissima*, a native of Timor in the East Indies. Its sting can reportedly last for up to twelve months if it doesn't kill you first.) Actually, the mechanics of the nettle sting are fascinating, and a good deal more complicated than you might think.

A nettle leaf and stem are covered with microscopic stiff hairs that can puncture skin at a touch. Until recently, they were thought to do their painful dirty work by injecting formic acid (the same stuff that red ants and bees employ), but research has now revealed that a multiple whammy of at least three chemicals is involved—a histamine to irritate the skin, acetylcholine to bring on a burning sensation, and hydroxytryptamine to encourage the other two. Both of the latter, incidentally, are nerve transmitter hormones also found in animals, which (as Paul Simons points out in *The Action Plant*) raises some curious questions about the boundary between animal and vegetable.

Various folk remedies for soothing nettle stings exist, but so far I have not found one that works for me. The classic is probably juice from a dock leaf, for which Simons offers a bit of scientific evidence: dock apparently contains chemicals that inhibit the action of hydroxytryptamine. I've tried this (it's unfortunately as easy to find a dock as a nettle around my garden), and Carol swears by it (it works in

Ireland), but I went right on stinging. Another putative remedy I've read about is the juice of jewelweed. I haven't seen a jewelweed since I left New England, however, although there are supposed to be a few around. Possibly another impatiens, perhaps a nice 'Congo Cockatoo,' might do just as well. The most radical proposal, which comes from a book called A Modern Herbal, suggests applying nettle juice to the nettle sting. This "affords instant relief." By the time you got the juice, you'd need it.

There seems to be a belief that approaching a nettle in a calm and fearless manner, as if it were an unfriendly dog, can save you from the prickles. "He which toucheth a nettle tenderly is soonest stung," observed John Lyly four hundred years ago, while another rhyme concludes, "Grasp it like a man of mettle, and it soft as silk remains." I shall leave the proof of this to others more leather-skinned, or less susceptible, than I. After all, these things demand prudence. A keeper at the Natural History Museum in London is supposed to have been stung by a nettle that had been pressed and mounted by Linnaeus two centuries before.

In the meantime, at Towerhill Cottage, forests of nettles are flourishing around the edges of the meadow and in the wood, particularly along the route of an old overgrown track that used to carry wagon traffic up to Coedangred Common. This is only to be expected; nettles demand phosphates, and phosphates accumulate in the soil where humans and animals deposit them over a long period of time—in gardens and churchyards, along roads, in places where creatures have lived and (especially) died and been buried. So in a way, nettles are more domesticated than most wild plants and bound to be our familiars whether we like it or not. They make terrific compost, and nothing is better than an old nettlebed as a place to put a new raspberry patch.

Nevertheless, I've still got a lot of nettles that I'd like to get rid of. Back in 1878, a gentleman wrote a plaintive note to *The Garden* explaining that he had a vast number of nettles growing under trees on his property and asked for suggestions about eradicating them. One respondent argued that if you mowed them to the ground five or six times during the growing season, "this wears them out." Another claimed that all you needed to do was to cut them down and dig over them shallowly. But why worry? "All who have plenty of luxuriant nettles may rest satisfied that they have some good land." This observation must have been of cold comfort to the nettle-beset fellow.

It was left to the well-known Victorian gardener, the Rev. Charles Wolley-Dod, to come up with a really constructive solution. He had plenty of nettles, growing so vigorously that "we have sometimes made walking sticks of them." Wolley-Dod's solution was to plant an interesting new polygonum in the midst of the nettles, thus overpowering them. It was called, he thought, *Polygonum sieboldii* (although he bought it under the name of *P. japonicum*), and he reported it "rejoicing in the cool, damp, open soil in which nettles generally grow." Facing up to the native inhabitants, "it quite holds its own, and gradually beats them. It grows seven or eight feet high . . ."

Now *Polygonum sieboldii*, otherwise known as *P. cuspidatum* (or, more recently, *Fallopia japonica*) is none other than the noted aggressor Japanese knotweed, which—we now know—spreads like wildfire and is almost impossible to eradicate. Poor Wolley-Dod. There is an old saw: "Better stung by a nettle than prickt by a rose." Or strangled by a knotweed, I'd say.

III

Some People

MISS WILLMOTT

❀

Plenty of plant names flatter their "discoverers" ("discovery"—like Columbus's "discovery" of America—being a relative thing), but a number of other labels are less obvious, even mysterious. Who, for example, was Joe Pye? Any suggestions about Jenny (of Creeping Jenny, *Lysimachia nummularia*) or Bet (of Bouncing Bet, *Saponaria officinalis*)? And what about William (regarded as Sweet)?

My favorite in this category of eponymous plant names must be Miss Willmott's Ghost, otherwise and more formally known as *Eryngium giganteum*, a tall thistlelike umbellifer with silvery-blue bracts, stems, and flowers. Viewed from a distance in the gloaming, it really does look ghostly, a sort of unearthly presence hovering over more modest flowers. Fair enough. But why Miss Willmott?

In life, Ellen Ann Willmott (1858–1934) was anything but ghostly. On the contrary, she was a splendid representative of English plutocracy at its most vigorous, a maiden lady who harbored a great admiration for Napoleon, a collector of rare books, and (regrettably) a terrific spendthrift. She was also—and this is why we remember her—a fanatic and brilliantly successful gardener. In the company of such great plantswomen as Gertrude Jekyll and Vita Sackville-West, Miss Willmott can claim a distinguished place.

While there have always been fine woman gardeners, it's interesting to see how during the eighteenth century, and still more during the nineteenth, gardening as a suitable occupation for a lady came to be acceptable, even worth encouraging. The cottage garden had always been the woman's province. When rich men got caught up in the fashion for creating grand landscape parks, planting trees, and excavating lakes, the job of looking after the flower gardens at the back of the house more often than not fell to their wives. In the nineteenth century, with villas replacing huge estates, the flowers staged a comeback. Many women—encouraged by writers like Jane Loudon with her *Gardening for Ladies* and *The Lady's Country Companion*—eagerly took charge, frequently becoming real experts in the process.

Thus Ellen Willmott's mother was a gardener; so was her sister Rose; and their comfortable circumstances offered plenty of scope for exercising their talents. Father was a self-made man, risen to wealth through his work as a lawyer and astute investments in property, and other moneyed family connections meant that Ellen was well-off from the start. She received an annual gift of a thousand pounds—equivalent to about $60,000 today—from her godmother. In 1876, the Willmotts settled at Warley Place, a handsome Queen Anne mansion in Essex, with gardens and a respectable piece of the surrounding countryside at their disposal.

While her parents lived, Ellen's gardening activity was enthusiastic without being excessive. In her early twenties, she got her father's permission to build an alpine rock garden (his one stipulation was that he shouldn't be able to see it from his study window) and created a deep rocky gorge fitted out with boulders, a stream, and a cave known as "the filmy-fern grotto." This was unique, a far cry from the carpet-bedding then fashionable on English lawns, and was later admired by connoisseurs like William Robinson and the alpine expert Reginald Farrer. The latter, who found it "to my own personal taste, a trifle too violent to be altogether pleasant," nevertheless caught the authentic Willmottian spirit in noting that it was "still a noble example of definite purpose definitely carried out."

There was certainly something very "definite" about Ellen Willmott. Her sister was to marry well, and eventually moved off to her husband's estate of Spetchley Park (he in time also inherited Berkeley Castle), but Ellen—despite her reported good looks—stayed single. Word was that she was a bit strong-minded, possibly even difficult. In any case, the Austenesque country round of dinner parties and garrison balls failed to produce a satisfactory husband. She took up painting and music (promptly acquiring no fewer than four priceless Amatis—a viola, a cello, and two violins), and dabbled in wood turning and photography. In 1888, her godmother died, leaving her £140,000 (more than $10 million in today's money).

Within a few years, both her parents dead, Ellen Willmott was mistress of Warley Place and a very rich woman. More and more, gardening became her chief diversion. She joined the Royal Horticultural Society and within a few years was elected to the Narcissus Committee, apparently on the strength of hybridizing work she had been carrying out on *Narcissus pseudonarcissus*, *N. pallidiflorus*, *N. campernelli*, and others. This brought her into contact with the leaders of the English gardening community, who began to sing the praises of Warley Place. "It seems to me," wrote George Wilson of Wisley (the estate that would later form the RHS's own gardens), "that your garden is the happiest combination of alpine, herbaceous and florist flowers I have ever seen."

If that was not enough, however, Miss Willmott now poured money, into two more grand establishments, with gardens—and costs—to match. The family had paid regular visits to Aix-les-Bains in the 1880s, and Ellen so loved the place that she decided to buy and develop a house called Tresserve on a hillside overlooking Lac Bourget. Here roses and more tender plants could flourish, and she purchased them in vast quantities, price no object. A single shipment from a nurseryman in Cork consisted of four hundred pounds of bulbs. Her biographer Audrey le Lièvre notes that in 1893, the order for one month alone from her dealer in Geneva ran to four quarto-sized pages with the entries in small handwriting, including many rare and exotic varieties. In its heyday, Tresserve had eleven thousand rose trees.

The other drain on the Willmott capital, a house called Boccanegra, was located on the Ligurian Coast of Italy near Ventimiglia. She bought this in 1905, intrigued by the possibilities it offered for growing still more and different kinds of Mediterranean plants. Carefully planned, yet appearing to be almost wild, Boccanegra's gardens cascaded down a steep rocky slope along old rain-cut channels; a major expense was in building reservoirs to supply water to the desperately thirsty plants. Here too came shipments of rare and unusual varieties culled from the collections of nurseries up and down the French and Italian Riviera, also in wholesale quantities. Le Lièvre estimates an expense of £2,000 ($160,000 today) for the garden during its first four years. And then there was the house to furnish and fill with books and *objets*.

It was while outfitting Boccanegra that the first intimations of financial troubles showed themselves. Bills were not paid on time; tradesmen (hesitantly, no doubt) began to complain. They were easy to ignore. After all, Miss Willmott had other things on her mind—the new Charron limousine, complete with Mozambiquean driver; the problem of timing her visit to each of her houses so to be there for the peak blooming period (or, in the case of Boccanegra, to avoid the mosquitoes); the difficulty of finding dependable staff to maintain not only the houses but the gardens in the meticulous style she demanded. On top of everything else, in 1907, a terrible fire gutted Tresserve, which was uninsured, and the rebuilding costs were crushing. In that year, she took out a loan of £15,000 ($1.2 million today) to see her through.

Meanwhile, very serious horticultural and botanical work was going on. One hundred and four gardeners labored at Warley, dressed in their uniforms of straw boaters with a green band, knitted green silk tie, and blue apron. The gardens, remarkable as they already were, required expanding; new plants were arriving from dealers and by exchange with private growers and botanical gardens all over the world (the Arnold Arboretum sent her a collection of hawthorns before they had even been named). Plant hunters produced more: an investment in the early expeditions of E. H. Wilson in China brought her lilies, rhododendrons, and seeds of *Paeonia delavayi*, as well as rare roses. According to botanical historian W. T. Stearn, by means of cash or persuasion she managed to acquire virtually every possible variety of certain genera, including ivies, irises, and roses. Dozens of plants were encouraged to flower for the first time in cultivation at Warley, and now bear either her name or the name of the garden. Among them are the parahebe 'Miss Willmott', *Primula warleyensis*, Rosa 'Ellen Willmott', *Rosa ×warleyensis*, and too many others to name.

Roses were undoubtedly her greatest delight. Her collections at Warley and Tresserve were famous and inspired the vast scholarly undertaking that would speed the way to financial disaster. Conceived of as a comprehensive descriptive illustrated monograph, *The Genus Rosa* occupied her energies and much of her income for at least a decade before 1910, when the first of its twenty-five parts was published. She never quite got the taxonomic details right—understandably, given that she lacked formal training and was unfamiliar with the new work on botanical genetics—and she failed to supply the kind of scientific apparatus indispensable to a modern monograph. But in the end she produced a beautiful book with specially commissioned paintings, and managed by dint of great persistence (and a long-suffering publisher) to sell some copies of it. Now rare, it is regarded as the twentieth-century counterpart of Redouté and Thory's *Les Roses*.

Already rendered shaky by her unstoppable extravagances, Miss Willmott's finances received one blow after another. Her father's old firm went bankrupt, and banks became less understanding as borrowings increased. Boccanegra was leased out, later sold. Cutbacks took place at Warley, concealed in part by the advent of World War I, and tenants had to be found for some of the subsidiary houses. (With one tenant, a Lady Angela Forbes—otherwise known as the first woman to have conducted her own divorce in a Scottish court—a rip-roaring battle ensued when Miss Willmott accused her of destroying a collection of species roses.) The gardens began losing their immaculate look. The end of the war, however, saw no revival in the Willmott fortunes, and in 1920, faced with the horrible prospect of leasing or selling Warley itself, she accepted a lowly offer for Tresserve. Warley and its gardens remained, but the shadows were closing in.

Now in her sixties, Ellen Willmott did her best to keep things going. Dressed in her usual old brown serge skirt, sabots, and a serge jacket, she worked outdoors every day with her sadly reduced gardening staff. She took long walks through the surrounding country, as she always had, going down to London for concerts and meetings of the RHS. A point of pride, never forgotten, was to pick an unusual blossom for her buttonhole, as a botanical puzzle for her fellow RHS committee members. Money became still tighter, and trips to London often involved taking some treasure to be quietly sold, a book or a bit of jewelry. (Not that everything went; a Sotheby's auction catalogue after her death listed many rare books and manuscripts, including herbals and florilegia and the manuscript of Henry Purcell's only violin sonata.) Paranoia crept in. Convinced that robbers were lurking, she put tripwires in the daffodils and took to carrying a loaded revolver in her reticule.

Against the odds, parts of the garden—the orchid house, the alpine glen, the walled garden with its roses—were kept up. She took on some pupils (one of whom later designed Hitler's garden at Berchtesgaden), and a few visitors continued to come. The orchid house closed in 1929. Finally, in 1935, after catching pneumonia in the course of one of her walks, Miss Willmott died. The total value of her estate was officially declared to be £12,787. No relatives were interested in the house or its gardens. They were sold off, demolished, and vandalized. Warley Place is now a nature reserve.

And Miss Willmott's Ghost? The story is that the *Eryngium giganteum* was her favorite flower and that it got its nickname because she liked to sow pinches of seed in neighbors' gardens on her walks. This strikes me as a bit unlikely, if only because she was obviously fonder of a great many more delicate—and welcome—plants. Still, as has been observed, the prickles are appropriate, and so is the eryngium's forthright and uncompromising stance. If the name helps us remember Ellen Ann Willmott, fine.

THE *FINDER* FOUNDER

❦

For any gardener in Britain past the stage of poached-egg plant and approaching modest horticultural sophistication, there's only one way to go: buy a copy of the chunky little paperback (978 closely packed pages in the 1997–98 edition) called *The Plant Finder*. Say you want a *Davidia involucrata* var. *vilmoriniana*. You could try West China, but *The Plant Finder* offers fifteen nurseries right here in Britain. Or a nice *Ophiopogon intermedius parviflorus*? Available (at a price) from a nursery in Yorkshire. It even tells you where to buy a stinging nettle (at Tivoli Garden, Ltd., in Salisbury, specialists in English wildflowers), if you happen to be silly enough to want to pay for one.

Along with W. J. Bean's classic *Trees and Shrubs Hardy in the British Isles* and a very few other books, *The Plant Finder* has become, in the dozen years of its existence, as essential to the serious British gardener as his trowel. Unrivaled as a shopping guide, it is now near to being the last word on the proper nomenclature and spelling of more than seventy thousand garden plants, both species and cultivars. Yet it is the brainchild and creation of a man who by his own admission "knows buggerall about botany" and does almost no gardening. In fact, according to his companion Denys Gurewoult, Chris Philip is best at spraying weeds. "I plant and he kills," says Gurewoult.

Sitting in the sunny conservatory of Lakeside near Worcester, above the sloping lawns and the dark little lake that gives the house its name, Philip told me how it all had fairly unexpectedly happened. The two men moved here from London in 1984, buying the property from a well-known daffodil breeder named Michael Jefferson Brown. For twenty-two years, Brown had been fixated on daffodils, bothering to plant almost nothing else, and when he and his bulbs departed, the garden—which ran to nearly six acres—was virtually bare. Philip and Gurewoult did what you or I would do. They assiduously visited other gardens on open days, peered over neighbors' fences, dug through garden books, and watched television gardening programs. Then they made a list of one hundred chosen plants, and traipsed off to garden centers to buy them.

It proved to be deeply frustrating. "We found about ten of those we wanted. The rest were either not available at all or the wrong cultivar." Wider searches turned up only a few more. It was at this point that Philip got his big idea. He would send off for a lot of catalogues and put together a sort of finders' list.

"Fools rush in," he says, thinking back on how little he knew what he was getting into. (Not that his earlier career had been without challenges. Starting in television, he moved on to work as a theatrical agent. He then became Britain's largest importer of display fireworks, rounding off this episode with the authorship of his first book, a bibliography of books relating to fireworks.) On his side, however, he had some knowledge of computers and databases. Learning that a group called the Hardy Plant Society already had a rudimentary list of plants and sources—about two thousand plants and a couple of hundred suppliers—maintained in a card file, he convinced them to let him computerize it and use it as the nucleus of his new database.

Then the responses from the nurseries they had circularized poured in, some four hundred of them, and Philip began entering the information into his computer. The format adopted—which is still in use—gives the genus name of the plant followed by species and cultivars arranged alphabetically, and up to thirty nurseries (in coded abbreviations) that stock each of them. (If more than thirty have it, it is said to be "widely available.") What had seemed straightforward, however, quickly turned into a snarl. "That's when I realized what I had let myself in for."

The plant names and taxonomy wholly lacked consistency. Philip told Gurewoult to take some reference works and make sense of it. "I spent three days on three entries," Gurewoult recalls, "and was no farther ahead than when I started. I went round and round in circles. Depending on which authority you chose, spellings, synonyms, everything was different."

What they had run into was something that would plague the first few editions of *The Plant Finder* (and by extension annoy gardeners forced to use new names), but which would in the end justify the publication in a way no one could have anticipated at the start. For some forty years, sound taxonomic revisions and decisions about names had been accumulating in the technical literature, but few had made their way into popular reference works for gardeners. Instead, there was a mixture: common names (often varying regionally), updates both accurate and inaccurate, old-fashioned usages, and simple mistakes (often the most jealously preserved). Part of the problem was the lack of a publication sufficiently broad based, frequently revised, and widely distributed among ordinary gardeners. Willy-nilly, *The Plant Finder* filled the bill.

Philip, however, was clearly in need of expert help, and by a stroke of extreme good fortune got it. The president of the Hardy Plant Society suggested he get in touch with a photographer, writer, and all-round plantsman named Tony Lord, who was then serving as Garden Adviser to the National Trust. Today, more than a decade later, Lord is still editing the guide, having proved to be, in Philip's words, "a tower of strength with an encyclopedic knowledge of every plant there is."

Leafing through *The Plant Finder*, you can see why such knowledge would be necessary. Thousands upon thousands of Latin names had to be sorted out and established as correct, a process that invited controversy. To begin with, protests were vociferous; Lord was accused of making name changes for the sheer malicious fun of it. In fact, the changes solely reflect official judgments. The greatest ker-fuffle occurred when our familiar garden chrysanthemums suddenly metamorphosed into dendranthemums, but *The Plant Finder* was simply following accepted taxonomic practice (and soon will follow it back again on the basis of a new decision by the authorities to restore the name). Fortunately, major revisions are now largely complete, with the exception of a few genera such as *Saxifraga* and *Salix*. "But they can be sorted out," Lord says optimistically.

The first edition of *The Plant Finder*, containing listings for twenty thousand plants and two hundred nurseries in the United Kingdom and Ireland, came out in 1987. Philip printed ten thousand in spite of predictions that the project was not financially viable and would be of little interest to gardeners. He sold 9,500 of them. Since then, he has issued a new edition each year, adding more and more plants and nurseries, until now the coverage totals more than 70,000 plants and 560 nurseries. Accuracy is a keynote. Plenty could go wrong—there are all those Latin names waiting to be misspelled, and symbols denoting everything from "Royal Horticultural Society Award of Garden Merit" to "new or amended synonym" to be misplaced. Cross-references abound. Yet such is the care devoted to getting things right that *The Plant Finder* is now a primary authority on plant names for gardeners and specialists here and abroad.

It also splendidly serves its first purpose as a means of locating hard-to-find plants. This has caused some controversy too. One disgruntled commentator deplored what he called "list lust," the tendency of some gardeners and nurseries to attempt to grow everything, thereby homogenizing the plant populations of the world. (This strikes me as a fairly recherché complaint, because many favorite plants come from someplace else. But it's a nice phrase.)

Three years ago, Philip—by then a rubicund sixty-five-year-old—realized that he had to make some provision for the continuation of publication. The RHS was the logical home for it, being (unlike Kew) concerned primarily with garden plants and cultivars. He struck a deal, agreeing to go on publishing until the RHS was ready to take over, which happened in 1996. Tony Lord continues to be editor, but he now has additional backup in the form of a high-powered RHS Advisory Panel on Nomenclature and Taxonomy to make difficult decisions on plant names. Perhaps the biggest problem currently faced by *The Plant Finder* is how to get everything in, what with the constant growth in the number of available plants and growers. The type can't get much smaller, and at a thousand pages it's beginning to look more like a brick than a book.

Once again, perhaps, Chris Philip may have the answer. When the RHS took over the book, he retained the right to use the database and has now expanded it into a CD-ROM containing not only *The Plant Finder* but an amazing array of other horticultural source materials.

Meanwhile, for those of us as yet inadequately computerized, there's the book. Except for sentimental reasons, I'll probably never want an *Elliottia pyroliflorus*, but if I do, thanks to *The Plant Finder*, I now know that it is called *Cladothamnus* and that the only place in Britain I can get one is the Starborough Nursery in Edenbridge, Kent.

JAGADIS CHUNDER BOSE

❧

I don't go out of my way to look for oddballs in the world of gardening, but it does seem to me sometimes that there are a lot of them around. Fanatics of one sort or another, pursuers of nonexistent truths, propagandists for solely owned theories—you can find them all. Still, one man's crank is another man's genius. I'm still not quite sure where to place Sir Jagadis Chunder Bose, and I gather I'm not alone in my indecision.

Bose—and I call him by his surname alone with some reluctance—is usually referred to as a botanist, although his real expertise lay elsewhere, in plant physiology, or physics, or possibly electrodynamics. (He also had a fair line in theosophical metaphysics, but so far as I know this did not play a major role in his scientific activities.) What he is known for, so far as he is known at all these days, are his attempts to demonstrate that plants can respond to stimuli the same way that other living organisms, from jellyfish to humans, can—indeed (to put it crudely), that plants have feelings.

Now this may smack of that notorious volume of pseudoscience published a few years ago, *The Secret Life of Plants,* and it is certainly significant that Peter Tompkins and Christopher Bird, its authors, include in it an exhaustive (if uncritical) account of Bose's career and work. Bose was nevertheless a serious scientist. Born in what is now

Bangladesh in 1858, he took his first degree at Calcutta University and then did postgraduate work in experimental physics at London University and Cambridge, mostly tinkering with the newly discovered radio waves. Some admirers claim he could have beaten Marconi to the wireless telegraph had he not refused to patent his own device. In one demonstration in Calcutta, he succeeded in transmitting a signal through three walls (and the corpulent chairman of the meeting) to set off a bell, fire a pistol, and detonate a small bomb.

In India, Bose taught and continued his experimental work. One day he noticed an odd phenomenon: a metal part in one of his radio receivers became "tired" with use, and then slowly recovered. Pursuing this notion, Bose was soon claiming that various metals could suffer fatigue and then be restored by the metallic equivalent of gentle massage or a warm bath; you could even "poison" a metal and then bring it back to life with an antidote. Papers presenting these findings in Paris and London were, according to his admiring biographer, "highly appreciated."

It was at this point that Bose began thinking about plants. If animals and metals, at the extremes of "living" and "nonliving," could be shown to share behavioral characteristics, then what he called "the vast expanse of the silent life of plants" ought to be explored. "Full of this idea," he rushed out of his London lodging, collected chestnut leaves, and subjected them to his usual test involving electrical stimulation and measurement of reactions. They responded vigorously. So did the carrots and turnips he tried next, although a sample of sea-kale was inert; this mystery was solved when the greengrocer admitted that it had been snowed on. Clearly, he concluded, all matter was intimately related, "a multiform unity in the great ocean of being."

Bose discovered more and more similarities between the reactions of plants and animals challenged by various stimuli. He administered poisons of different kinds, showing that the curve of response in the plants was remarkably similar to that in animal muscle. He made plants "fatigued" and measured how long and in what way they recovered. He put plants to sleep with chloroform and woke them up again. He even managed to transplant a large pine tree under anaesthesia, claiming that it did not suffer the usual shock.

Until now, Bose had been held in high, if wary, respect by the panjandrums of European science, but his reputation was due for a setback. Presenting the results of his startling findings before the august Royal Society in London in June 1901, he was attacked from an unexpected quarter. Sir John Burdon Sanderson, the foremost British expert on plant responses, had continued Darwin's researches on the physiology of the Venus's-flytrap, discovered electrical nervelike activity in the plant, and might have been expected to be sympathetic. He was not. Bose, he declared, had no business interfering in fields in which he lacked competence, such as physiology. His paper should not be published. Other senior figures concurred; the paper was relegated to the archives.

Were they fair? Probably not entirely. To some extent, Sanderson was acting out of pique because he had been upstaged. Some of what Bose proposed was plainly off the wall, although not all; he had, and continued to have, such distinguished supporters as Sir Sidney Vines, then president of the Linnean Society, and the philosopher–scientist Herbert Spencer. His rhetoric did him no particular good, larded as it was with cosmic notes about "the thrill in matter," nor did his deliberate attempt to breach the boundaries between established disciplines gain him friends. Worst of all—although no one was so rude as to say so—was the color of his skin. He was, after all, an Indian. As one hostile animal physiologist, later a convert, told him, "I thought your Oriental imagination had led you astray."

Shocked and offended, Bose fought back in the laboratory, devising new experiments and producing papers at a great rate. He now concentrated on studying plant responses, employing his favorite *Mimosa pudica* ("the sensitive plant," which has the happy habit of reacting instantly to being touched by drooping and folding up its leaves), along with *Desmodium gyrans*, the telegraph plant, an Indian species that moves its leaves up and down like a semaphore. His aim was to devise ways of telling how a plant *felt* under different conditions. How would it react to a specific stimulus if it was in an excited state? A depressed state? Dying? The trick was to invent instruments capable of registering and recording what were often extremely subtle and elusive reactions, to make plants produce (as he later put it) their "autographs."

In spite of trips back from Calcutta for demonstrations and lectures, Bose did not get along well with the English scientific establishment. The Linnean Society accepted a paper, but the Royal Society continued obdurate, and he eventually began publishing his own reports of his work in a long parade of diagram-filled books. *Response in the Living and the Non-Living* appeared in 1902, followed by *Plant Response as a Means of Physiological Investigation, Researches on the Irritability of Plants, Life Movements in Plants* (in three volumes), *The Nervous Mechanism of Plants, Plant Autographs and Their Revelations*, and more. With patience and a willingness to overlook repetition, it is possible to trace in them Bose's wonderful adventures along the border between plant and animal.

One series of experiments, for example, established that the skins of grapes, tomatoes, frogs, tortoises, and lizards "behave substantially alike," and that the digestive systems of insect-eating plants worked the same way as the stomachs of various animals. Using an array of Rube Goldberg devices to magnify responses, potentially as much as one hundred million times (so he claimed), he measured the reaction of plants to irritation (being rubbed with a piece of cardboard, shocked with electricity, struck sharply); to being drugged with alcohol, chloroform, and other substances (some suffered hangovers); and to being heated or chilled. He produced death spasms and discovered that when plant tissue died, it produced an electric discharge. (A half-pea, he calculated, could give off as much as half a volt, so a pan of five hundred pairs of half-peas, suitably hooked up in series, would be enough to electrocute the cook!) He made tendrils of climbing plants coil on demand with the help of electricity and studied the phenomenon of memory in plants, suggesting that they could be trained to respond to particular stimuli. And while sensitive plants like the mimosa were his chosen subjects, he also worked with vegetables normally regarded as hopelessly inactive. About 1914, the *Nation* magazine ran the following tongue-in-cheek report after a visit to Bose's London laboratory:

> *In a room near Maida Vale there is an unfortunate carrot strapped to the table of an unlicensed vivisector. Wires pass through two glass tubes full of a white substance; they are like two legs, whose feet are buried in the flesh of the carrot. When the vegetable is pinched with a pair of forceps, it winces. It is so strapped that its electric shudder of pain pulls the long*

arm of a very delicate lever which actuates a tiny mirror. This casts a beam of light on the frieze at the other end of the room, and thus enormously exaggerates the tremor of the carrot. A pinch near the right-hand tube sends the beam seven or eight feet to the right, and a stab near the other wire sends it as far to the left. Thus can science reveal the feelings of even so stolid a vegetable as the carrot.

Bose was particularly proud of his machines and reproduced detailed drawings in his books showing how they were constructed. One, which he called the Crescograph, was actually capable of indicating—on the spot—just how fast or slow a plant was growing, and he could use it to measure the effect of short-term factors like a flash of light. (The flash apparently jolted the plant; weak radio waves speeded growth, strong ones slowed it.) Other devices helped him explore how some plants "sleep," exhibiting a pattern of "awareness" and "insensibility" through the course of the day ("Mimosa is a late-riser").

Bose was so convinced that plants had nerves—they certainly behaved as though they did—that he spent much time and energy trying to find one. He finally concluded that he had isolated nerve tissue in a fern stalk. The mimosa, he was sure, was likewise equipped, but the "phloem-strand" in question couldn't be removed "without tearing it to pieces." As Brent Elliott notes in a recent article on Bose, "Subsequent researchers have not been persuaded."

Today, seventy or eighty years on, much of Bose's work has been overtaken by complexities of knowledge and information that I would hesitate to discuss even if I were able. To the extent that he was utterly convinced of his own rightness—he almost never made use of anyone else's discoveries or built on related research, meanwhile scrupulously ignoring competing evidence—he prejudiced his case, and drifted further and further from the scientific mainstream. Yet according to a recent book by Paul Simons, *The Action Plant*, in certain important ways Bose deserves more respect than he has received. Sir Jagadis, Simons points out, "was the first person to appreciate fully that electrical signals control leaf movements in [mimosa]," and succeeded in showing that "plant excitability has much in common with animal nerves." Now that's not quite as sensational as proving that your rhododendron can be as affectionate as your cat, but it sounds to me like perfectly plausible science.

GEOFF

❦

Until his sad and sudden death at the age of only fifty-nine recently, the best-known gardener in Britain was not Penelope Hobhouse or Christopher Lloyd, but a man most American garden buffs had never even heard of, an ordinary-looking chap with a slightly twisted grin and a Middle England accent named Geoff Hamilton. On Friday night prime-time television, in half a dozen books (virtually every one a best-seller), in up to five magazine pieces a month, Geoff was practically ubiquitous. Indications were that if anybody could think of another way to package him, most of the gardening public in this country would have happily bought in.

Most, but not quite all, which was what made him particularly interesting to anyone (like me) fascinated by what I'm forced to call the sociology of British gardening. There exists here a distinct divide, running along fault lines of class and economic standing, right through the gardening world. On one side is a sort of hereditary peerage of experts and proprietors of old and famous gardens, what you might call an aristocracy of the spade. Until recently, the Royal Horticultural Society belonged to them. Some write books, others merely grace the countryside with their creations. Their numbers, as with other aristocracies, are shrinking. On the other side, infinitely more numerous, is everybody else: newcomers to gardening, heirs of the cottage traditions or workingmen's clubs, city folk keeping up their back gardens, allotment gardeners. Geoff Hamilton spoke to them.

He also, I found, after watching his half-hour weekly programs with steadily increasing loyalty over several years, spoke to me. A few months before his death, he invited me to pay him a visit on his home ground a couple of hours north of London. Here in the country—very flat East Midlands country—he lived in a nicely renovated old house called Barnsdale, up a muddy and totally unmarked lane. The obscurity was purely a matter of self-defense. If he had ever held a GARDEN OPEN day, fifty thousand Geoff Hamilton fans might well have shown up. After all, the core viewership of his weekly television program *Gardeners' World* was 3.5 to 4 million, and as many as 6 million settled down to watch parts of his last BBC series, *The Cottage Garden*. And that's not even counting the one hundred thousand or so who bought copies of the tie-in book.

Alerted to my arrival by a shout from a gardener, Hamilton descended from his workroom in an outbuilding, and we sat down at the kitchen table to talk. Just then— late autumn—was what passed for a relaxing time in his yearly schedule. Broadcasts were over for the winter. He had nothing to do but prepare for *Gardeners' World* and the next series, write another book, write one of his weekly pieces for *Radio Times* or the *Daily Express*, or a monthly one for *Country Living* or *Gardener's World* magazine, supervise the gardeners (three to four full-time) working in the gardens and the greenhouse, sleep, eat . . . Not surprisingly, he had suffered a moderate heart attack about a year before the massive one that finally struck him down (during a charity bicycle ride in South Wales), and he was in theory supposed to be slowing down.

In person, Hamilton was exactly the same as his television image—amiable, enthusiastic, faintly keyed-up, the
sort of fellow you'd be fortunate to have as a next-door
neighbor willing and able to give you tips on cultivating asparagus and help you balance a ladder or share a load of manure.
He came across as knowledgeable, but not intimidatingly so,
which was one obvious reason for his success. "I have to show
authority, of course, but I also have to appear to be learning.
That's the problem with gardening television shows in this
country. Getting the level right is a constant dilemma. In the
end you have to make a program for yourself."

The sort of program Hamilton made for himself—and
they were his ideas, planned and scripted by him—clearly
reflected his interests and background. You wouldn't find
him wandering through Sissinghurst commenting languidly
on the *Rosa longcuspis* or comparing *Carya illinoiensis* with
C. myristiciformis (in Latin). Instead, in smartly paced and
neatly photographed sequences, he showed you how to
build a compost bin out of clapboards, or gave planting
advice for a parterre that would fit into an urban back garden. His *Cottage Garden* series demonstrated the construction of two complete gardens, one on a budget (the
"Artisan's Garden"), the other a "Gentleman's" version—
but both small, and both perfectly practical projects for the
average staffless gardener. And while the level of advice was
(to this American anyway) fairly sophisticated, it was hardly addressed to what Hamilton calls "the Rosemary Vereys
of this world"—those gardeners on the upper side of the
great divide.

Given Hamilton's background, it's unlikely that it ever
would have been. Born and brought up in the Lea Valley on
London's northern edge, he was always interested in gardens
and plants. His father, a keen gardener but no expert, want-

ed him to go to university and become a scientist, but he held out for agricultural school and ended up studying horticulture at a college in Essex. Claiming that he "always wanted to work with my hands, outdoors," he got his wish, but life as a graduate turned out to be tough, consisting of heavy labor landscaping and in nurseries. "I had just about no skills or talents at all."

What he had instead was luck. "There must be this lady above the clouds who is always saying, 'Let's give him a break,'" Hamilton recalled. The break this time was getting to know the editor of *Garden News*, a popular weekly, who asked him to write a piece on landscape gardening. After agonies of composition (at one point the editor despairingly announced, "Oh Christ, I can't use this") Hamilton eased up, got his article in shape, and realized he liked writing. Years as a contributor followed, then a staff job, then the editorship of a monthly magazine called *Practical Gardening*, at the loamy heart of Britain's thriving horticultural media community.

The gardening press, comprising roughly a dozen weekly and monthly magazines plus uncounted newspaper and magazine columns, is profitable and influential here; combined monthly circulation of the magazines alone is on the order of two million copies (for a population a fifth the size of the United States). But Hamilton, by then living in rural Rutland, was not getting rich, and jumped at the chance to audition for a television gardening program. He got the job—the test interview involved discussing garden gnomes with a gentleman who had just been celebrating the birth of a new baby with an alcoholic lunch, and Hamilton hardly needed to open his mouth. And although that program soon folded, he managed to meet the producer of *Gardeners' World*, the BBC's flagship garden show, who hired him on the spot. His first series for GW was typical of what was to follow. He had just rented a couple of acres that once held a garden and was now totally overgrown; the series showed Hamilton clearing it and bringing it back to life. (The clearing part actually involved bulldozing the site because filming had to start in two months and there was no time to spare. They didn't show that.)

In 1979, Hamilton moved up to be principal presenter of *Gardeners' World* (he would take over as chief in 1984), marking the promotion with a huge new mortgage and the purchase of Barnsdale, which he promptly began turning into a sort of horticultural back lot. The initial enterprise was to move his old garden, plant by plant and shrub by shrub, to the meadow behind his new quarters. This was accomplished in a single week and conveniently provided the subject for a program on "How to Move a Garden." Improving the quality of the soil, which had been exhausted by centuries of farming, took much longer. It was still going on at the time of my visit, with the help of hundreds of tons of manure contracted for delivery annually by a neighboring farmer.

A gray November afternoon was not the best time to see anyone's garden, but despite much of it having "gone over," as Hamilton put it, I could see that Barnsdale would be lovely in a kinder season. There was no grand landscaping; in fact, the nearest thing to pretension was a long grass alley bordered by perennial beds with an urn at the far end. What we had instead were a number of smaller sections framed by fences and hedging and little copses of trees, interesting and well planted in themselves but hardly prepossessing. It was a bit unnerving to realize, when you spotted a familiar piece of latticework or a bricked walk, that most of the sections were actually leftover gardens built and filmed for one series or another. Hamilton kept them up; they might well have come in handy for some future production. Besides, he was a real hands-on gardener, and like the rest of us wanted to have the place looking good.

To maintain the right sophistication level of *Gardeners' World*, Hamilton claimed to keep in mind a hypothetical average viewer: "A 65- to 70-year-old widow who knows a bit about horticulture and how to use a hammer, saw, and screwdriver." He harbored no illusions about his own particular expertise or his relationship to what he viewed as the uppercrust portion of the gardening community. "I don't pretend to know a great deal about garden history or landscape design. You do pick up a lot, preparing programs. You work up what you need to know. After all, *Gardeners' World* is a journalist's job.

"On the other hand, Penelope Hobhouse and Rosemary Verey and those people are great artists, no question about it. But they're daunting. I can certainly learn things from them, and do. What worries me about them is that they give you the feeling that you ought to be able to do what they do and make you feel bad if you can't. I want to make gardening accessible. Surely the best idea is to broaden the base of the pyramid. We need the peak, as something to aspire to."

Hamilton was cheered by the fact that the RHS membership has "rocketed" recently, and was convinced that ordinary gardeners are changing the nature of what was formerly regarded as an exclusive club for gentlemen. "I used to have great battles with the RHS. I once wrote that it was out of touch with gardeners and a senior RHS person responded angrily: 'Who is this man Hamilton?' Having to ask that just proved how out of touch they really were. Another time one of the toffs complained that *Gardeners' World* had lost its way because we were 'always talking about potatoes.'" Perhaps better than most people, Hamilton knew that potatoes were exactly what his viewers wanted to talk about.

In any case, Geoff's heart was always with the authentic old English countryman gardener, the sort best typified by George Flatt, an 89-year-old Suffolk pensioner he was lucky enough to find for the *Cottage Garden* series. Flatt was unforgettable, talking as easily about his cabbages and apples in a broad East Anglian accent as if the cameraman and sound man were miles away. "George never took a blind bit of notice," Hamilton recalls. "I've never seen anyone so unconcerned about modern technology." And, like Hamilton himself, George knew his onions.

JOSEPH ROCK

❀

As plant hunters go, Joseph Rock could not be called a
lucky man. Disasters of one sort or another seemed to
dog his progress through life, leaving him more familiar
with frustration than triumph. On top of that, he suffered
from a bad stomach. This may go some way toward explaining why the editor of *National Geographic Magazine*, who
published several articles by Rock, pronounced him "one of
the most cantankerous of human beings."

It is a mournful fact, typical of the way Rock played hide
and seek with fame, that the most famous plant bearing his
name—*Paeonia suffruticosa* ssp. *rockii*, a rare and beautiful
tree peony—was not even his own discovery,* and his
introduction of the seeds passed almost unnoticed. Not for
Rock the cheers that greeted E. H. Wilson's *Lilium regale* or
Frank Kingdon-Ward's blue poppy. Although he spent more
than fifty years collecting plants, introducing no fewer than
493 species of rhododendron into the Western world (more

---

*Reginald Farrer may claim credit for first seeing it growing in the wild,
in China's Kansu Province in 1914. He apparently failed to collect
plants or seeds. Some time after 1925, Rock spotted the plant in a
lamasery garden in Choni in Kansu and sent seeds back to the Arnold
Arboretum. In 1928, the lamasery—and its gardens—were laid waste by
bandits, but by the late 1930s the peony (by then called *Paeonia suffruticosa* 'Joseph Rock' or 'Rock's Variety') had been flowered in several
countries.

than were known before, all told), as well as many kinds of berberis, meconopses, primulas, and potentillas, and collected thousands of valuable herbarium specimens, poor Rock never really hit it big.

Josef Franz Karl Rock was born in Vienna in 1884, and from the first evinced interest in unusual forms of scholarship. When he was ten, he started to learn Arabic, and by sixteen was teaching it. Chinese came next. Bridling at family plans to make him enter the priesthood, he set off for England, but—predictably—never got there; he missed the channel steamer at Antwerp and in a fit of enthusiasm booked passage to America instead.

Josef became Joseph. Wandering from place to place around the United States in search of a climate that would favor his weak chest, Rock picked up English in Texas and eventually arrived in Hawaii, where he gained both his health and a job teaching Latin and natural history. Up to this point, he had shown few signs of any interest in botany, much less expertise, but in 1908 he suddenly blossomed as the first-ever Botanical Collector for the Hawaiian Division of Forestry and began churning out an amazing number of learned articles and books on everything from trees to algae. To assist in the latter study, he convinced a rich local man to build him a glass-bottomed boat. He also found time to assemble an impressive herbarium and to take up American citizenship.

Being Rock, however, problems arose. The Forestry Division ran out of funds; he shifted to the College of Hawaii, where he taught and continued to clamber through the hills collecting. He was not happy teaching; his few students remembered him as "temperamental as a prima donna." Moody and private, he later admitted that he was "dreadfully lonely." Trips at his own expense to the Far East, and once around the world, cheered him a bit, but by 1920 he was ready to quit. The last straw was a decision to move his precious herbarium—by then some twenty-five thousand specimens—out of his control. Furious, he headed for the mainland to look for another job.

As his biographer S. B. Sutton observes, specialists in Hawaiian botany were not exactly in demand at the time. After several turndowns, however, he struck upon an opportunity that seemed likely to justify all his previously unrewarded efforts. The Office of Foreign Seed and Plant Introduction of the U.S. Department of Agriculture wanted someone to find the mysterious chaulmoogra tree, source of what promised to be the first effective cure for leprosy. Who better than Joseph Rock?

Although chaulmoogra nuts, from which the precious oil was drawn, had appeared in Thai and Burmese markets, the tree itself (*Taraktogenos kurzii*) proved elusive. Rumor placed it in the Doi Sootep Mountains west of Chiang Mai, but all Rock could find there were leeches and a number of gilded temples, which he photographed. Traveling first by boat and then overland through dense tropical forests ("inhabited by tigers, leopards and snakes," he noted) to Burma, he was advised by natives that the tree grew in the Kalama Range north of Moulmein. The tree in question, although a near relative, turned out to be the wrong one, so Rock pressed on. When he finally found *T. kurzii*, in jungle north of Mandalay, the first specimens were without nuts, but by scouring the countryside he at last got what he was looking for. He also got an unexpected bonus in excitement. His party was stalked by a man-eating tiger, which killed a village woman. With Rock's help the natives trapped it—using the woman's body as bait. Loaded with seeds of the chaulmoogra tree, Rock trekked back to civilization.

Unfortunately for him, although his adventure made good copy for the *Geographic* (once his text had been rewritten by the long-suffering editors), it soon developed that the chaulmoogra oil he had gone to so much trouble to find was not a miracle cure for leprosy after all. It worked in some cases, but the side effects were insupportable, and researchers moved on to other treatments. Poor Rock had to move on too. Still supported by the USDA, he traveled north to hunt for plants in China proper, finally settling in the town of Likiang in the western province of Yunnan where he would spend most of the rest of his life.

Here he collected in earnest—tens of thousands of plant specimens, more thousands of bird and mammal skins—and explored the mountains and valleys on the borders of Tibet. It was great country for rhododendrons and primulas, although the cream had already been skimmed by such predecessors and competitors as George Forrest, Kingdon-Ward, Wilson, and the French botanist–priests Jean Pierre Armand David and Jean Marie Delavay. With his command of Chinese, and the local dialects which he could soon speak, Rock recruited assistants and established relationships with local potentates like the King of Muli. Support from various American sources—the Arnold Arboretum and the National Geographic Society in particular—kept him going year by year.

And he needed the money. He was never one to suffer in the field. When he went on an expedition, he normally moved in some state, with a train of horses and carriers. His equipment included a folding bathtub from Abercrombie & Fitch, and he made a practice of dressing for dinner, which was prepared to his orders by a specially trained cook and consumed with silver cutlery from china laid on a linen-covered table. His rationale for such luxury was "face." As he once remarked, "You've got to make people believe you're someone of importance if you want to live in these wilds." That may not have been overstating the case: Rock's diaries are full of stories of marauding warlord armies, brigands, renegade armed priests, and general disorder. More than once his plans were disrupted by fighting, political and otherwise, which deeply offended his Austrian sense of civil propriety.

In 1927, a funding crisis arose with the death of Charles Sargent, Rock's main backer at the Arnold Arboretum. In the nick of time, he managed to secure a commission from the National Geographic Society to explore unmapped mountains west of Likiang. One expedition almost became a disaster when an unseasonable hailstorm destroyed barley crops and the natives blamed it on the Rock party; they had been circling the sacred mountains in a counterclockwise direction, which every good Tibetan knows is blasphemous. But it was during this trip that Rock got his first glimpse of an enormous mountain called Minya Konka. Could it be the highest mountain in the world?

In March 1929, confident that this time he had made a seriously important discovery, Rock set off on an expedition with National Geographic Society backing to find out. Minya Konka—which he later diplomatically renamed Mount Grosvenor in honor of the president of the Society—had been seen and reported before from a distance, but never measured. Climbing it was out of the question, so Rock took bearings from surrounding high points with a variety of instruments before reaching his triumphant conclusion. "MINYA KONKA HIGHEST PEAK ON GLOBE 30250 FEET ROCK," said the cable to the Society. As it turned out, it wasn't. Rock's enthusiasm had run away with him again. Mount Grosvenor, while a considerable protuberance, was in fact roughly a mile shorter than Rock's calculation, and no rival to Everest.

Rock might be excused not noticing the Wall Street crash, but it had a direct effect on his income. Moreover, the editors of the *Geographic* were getting restive. "Imagination he has none. Or form," wrote one bedeviled rewrite man. "Apparently he has never learned to write with a view to holding reader interest . . ." Possibly because of this, his contributions (after one leaden effort entitled "Konka Risumgongba: Holy Mountain of the Outlaws") ceased. Plant collecting and exploring (on a reduced stipend) continued, but more and more Rock focused on his main interest, the ethnology of the Na-khi people living in the region around Likiang.

Floods, roaming hordes of leaderless soldiers, inflation, toothaches—all these made Rock's life unpleasant. He even fell back on speculating in currency, and of course lost money. The approach of war unsettled him completely. Three times he packed up his entire huge library and shipped it to Dalat in French Indochina, only to ship it back to Likiang again. His luck did not improve. Plates for one major work were destroyed by Japanese bombs at a printer in Shanghai, while all his notes and manuscripts—the fruit of twelve years of labor—went to the bottom when the ship carrying them to Europe was torpedoed. Yet apart from two years spent working for the U.S. Army Map Service in Calcutta, Rock stayed on in Likiang. He was still there in 1949, when the Communists chased him out for good, an unhappy man as usual. He retreated to Hawaii and devoted his last years to reconstructing his lost papers, including a Na-khi dictionary.

It isn't easy to get the measure of Joseph Rock as a plant hunter. Significantly, he never published so much as a single paper on Chinese plants, although he worked there for nearly half a century. Apart from the peony, gardeners know little of his introductions, yet on one trip alone he collected six thousand chestnut seedlings in hope of finding a blight-resistant variety. Hundreds of plant varieties bear his name. And in Likiang his memory as a plantsman lives on. In his book *Travels in China* (1989), Roy Lancaster tells of meeting a very old man there who remembered Rock. Because of ill health (that bad stomach?), Rock had employed villagers to hunt plants for him. But he was the only one who could tell them what to look for.

CANON ELLACOMBE

❦

Given a facility for writing sermons (and they didn't have to be either long or learned), life as a village rector in nineteenth-century England must have been enviable. If you were a gardener, so much the better. No doubt you already occupied the nicest house for miles around, probably a comfortable old vicarage surrounded by two or three acres of land and a collection of ancient trees. Money was usually no problem—you could call on local help when you needed your lawn scythed or your shrubs pruned. In fact, wrote Henry Ellacombe, "A country parson without some knowledge of plants is surely as incomplete as a country parsonage without a garden. . . . Such a man must be wretched . . . but I have not much pity for him."

Canon Ellacombe had a right to feel superior. Amid a galaxy of clergyman–gardeners, he was outstanding, a plantsman whose reputation had, by the time of his death in 1916 at an age approaching one hundred, far outgrown the confines of his modest garden in a Gloucestershire village.

Part of Ellacombe's fame stemmed from his achievements as a gardener—he was an expert horticulturist responsible for collecting and growing many rarities and new varieties. But at least as much may be laid to his books, particularly the small classic called *In a Gloucestershire Garden*, first published in 1895. Packed with wise observations, comments on plants, aphorisms, and attractive moralities, it combines a fresh and easy prose style with the stuff of nostalgia, serving to fix, as if in amber, the very essence of a parsonage garden a century ago.

Except for his years at Oxford and a short period as a curate in Derbyshire, Henry Ellacombe spent his entire life in Bitton, a tiny village between Bristol and Bath.* His father—a scholarly expert on bell-ringing and by all accounts a considerable gardener—was vicar there, and had started the garden that his son inherited. (An old document dated 1830 lists no less than 208 different roses grown by Ellacombe's father.) "I have in mind," the Canon was to write, "a garden of small extent," and the famous garden was exactly that: only an acre and a half including the vegetable patch.

Universally known by his ecclesiastical title—which he received in 1881 when he was made an honorary canon of Bristol Cathedral—Ellacombe had what must be described as a deeply unexciting life. One searches in vain for a dramatic narrative. He married, his wife bore ten children, he made a regular habit of composing a set of Latin verses while resting before dinner (which he would then recite to the family and guests), he went on jaunts to the Continent with one or another of his children, he fished and hunted and collected plants. Before taking over from his father in 1850, he seems to have preferred genealogy to gardening, producing "beautiful paintings of coats of arms." In the words of one slightly despairing memoirist, "Full of interest and beauty as was his life, it was not eventful in the ordinary sense of the term."

While in this, I suspect, he was typical of many younger sons of the gentry who chose to enter the church, the

---

*Because of modern boundary shifting, Bitton is no longer in Gloucestershire, but in Avon.

Canon—as he makes plain from his book—found abundant excitement close to home, among his plants. He apparently had little or no interest in what he dismissed as the "artistic" side of gardening, but rather treasured the individual plant—its beauty, its health, its exact preferences as to placement and soil. Beyond that, he wanted to understand it botanically, and find out all he could about its natural history and its associations with humans. If necessary (and it usually was necessary, because he had absolutely no room to spare), a single specimen of a given variety would do, although he was as a rule determined to find a sample of every different kind available. "Each little flower meant so much to him," wrote the botanist W. J. Bean in his description of Bitton. "It would be impossible to find another garden of its size so rich in species and varieties of hardy flowers and shrubs. . . . The collector spirit held him to the very end."

So although it was "wholly devoid of design," Bitton represented an amazing concentration of rarities. Bean estimated that over the fifty years before his death, Ellacombe grew nearly three thousand different species or varieties there. In a single five-year period in the 1870s, he received about 4,900 plants and 1,000 packets of seeds from various private individuals and botanical gardens ranging from Kew to New York to Berlin and Gibraltar. Many found a home at Bitton, or at the very least had a good crack at growing in the limey earth and comfortable climate that prevailed there, sheltered between the Cotswolds and the Mendips.

In the days before specialist nurseries, such exchanges of plants were commonplace and did much to knit together the gardening community. Ellacombe was a great believer in sharing his rarities, on the principle that "no garden could flourish that was not constantly giving." He was on close terms with successive directors of Kew throughout much of his life, for example, and was proud to have supplied examples of nearly two dozen rare plants for illustration in Kew's magisterial *Botanical Magazine*. Yet there was not much of the cool and objective scientist about him. He did not hesitate to express his likes and dislikes, the latter of which were famously numerous. Those plants he rejected out of hand were alone said to be sufficient to fill a border. ("A border?" one acquaintance commented. "You'd be nearer the mark if you said an acre.") They included florist's tulips ("always coarse and flaring") and what he considered "the ugliest object of all," a bed of double zinnias.

Similarly, Ellacombe's favorite plants show a wonderful inconsistency, ranging from sentimental attachment to admired oddity. In her contribution to a collective memoir, the distinguished gardener Ellen Willmott (see p. 91) listed some of them. There was a black pansy brought from Italy by the Canon's father; *Statice cosirensis* (now *Limonium cosyrensis*) grown from seeds brought to England by a sailor who had been in the Bitton choir as a boy; a fine *Viburnum tomentosum* var. *mariesii* (now *V. plicatum*); *Fremontia californica* (which Ellacombe was the first to grow outdoors in England); a convolvulus said to have been raised from seeds found in the pocket of a drowned sailor; and a number of old roses, particularly one he called *Rosa hemisphaerica*. Other visitors to Bitton in springtime noted his one concession to display—a grand spread of *Anemone blanda* in all forms, including doubles that he was the first to record. Many wildlings get a good word from the Canon, although not the lesser celandine, which he regarded as "a sad weed." For someone so interested in unusual plants, he was at heart conservative, preferring old standard varieties, and often inveighed against unnecessary innovations.

In several ways, Ellacombe was ahead of his gardening time. Conifers were very fashionable in late Victorian England; he had "no great love for them." He believed in letting hardy plants fend for themselves: "I dislike all tyings and nailings, all sticks, and everything that tends to cramp the free growth of the plants." The modern practice of letting clematis clamber through and over shrubs and trees was old hat to him, and he argued for more climbers to be allowed to go where they would "by their own unassisted powers"—including several types of climbing asparagus!

Friends spoke of Ellacombe's "robust vitality." This could sometimes take a startling form. He once went on a trout-fishing and plant-collecting trip to Ireland, commenting in a letter home: "Went fishing by myself. It was not a good day, but I managed to get about five dozen." His usual response to the offering of a plant he didn't like the look of was "Throw it away!" Nor was a plant necessarily safe once planted in his own border. Suddenly annoyed by its appearance, he might pull it out bodily and discard it, only to replant another specimen later. Much as he loved to have visitors, claiming that Bitton could supply some special beauty in every season, indeed every month, he could be sharp with anyone whom he sensed was merely faking interest. When one lady simpered, "Oh, Canon Ellacombe, what do you do to have all these beautiful flowers?" he answered forthrightly. "Well, madam, I plant 'em."

Still, from his writings and from the recollections of his many friends, it is plain that Ellacombe was a lovable and much-loved man, happy in his garden and his well-used library. His wisdom was of a kind that has an engaging—and lasting—charm. "The garden," he wrote, "is a constant pleasure, and . . . the pleasure does not depend on unbroken success." And again: "The true gardener is never overmuch disquieted by bad seasons, whether they are seasons of frost or drought . . . Bad seasons are a trial of his faith." His three prerequisites for a gardener "wishing to have and keep a good collection of plants" are patience, liberality, and a catalogue.

Needless to say, the Canon possessed all three. He was past ninety when a visitor commented on his experiments with supposedly lime-loving rhododendrons just arrived from Edinburgh, having had no luck with rhododendrons in sixty years. (He refused to use peat, although Ashmore, his frustrated gardener, is supposed to have smuggled in a load in the dead of night on one occasion.) His staying powers as an elderly man were legendary. Well into his eighties, he delightedly reported hearing from a French doctor in Paris that "your heart is splendide; it does belong to a strong man of twenty." Continental jaunts became, if anything, more adventurous.

At the advanced age of eighty-one, Canon Ellacombe undertook to cross a remote Alpine pass on an equally elderly horse. It is pleasant to hold in mind this picture of the hale old fellow, recorded by the much younger friend who accompanied him:

> *We pushed on through deepish snow to the top of the next ridge, and on the other side we got into a tangle of torrents running through boulders and rhododendron scrub, and to add to our difficulties it thundered and rained for all it was worth. The Canon was quite placid, sitting on his horse as if he were part of it (it was often as not on its head or its knees!), a huge cotton umbrella over his head, and continually shouting, "Baker! Baker! What's that flower?"*

THE BISHOP'S GARDEN

❧

One of the least attractive expressions in the whole realm of gardening must be "plant material." Landscape architects use it all the time. Of course they are in the business of creating effects, not breeding pansies or coaxing a wisteria to bloom, so perhaps they can be excused. But talk of "plant material" has always struck me as a bit insulting to the plants themselves. How would you like to be referred to as "human material?"

I'm firmly on the side of the plantsman or woman: the person who evinces real affection for each of his or her charges, is curious about its likes and dislikes, treasures it in spite of its failings, and never thinks of it as "material." I'm glad to say that there are still plenty of gardeners like that around today, and probably always will be. But the true springtime of the plantsman, I am convinced, was some four hundred years ago, in the heart of the Renaissance. I'm led to this conclusion by a book I came across recently, a book about a book about a garden.

Hortus Eystettensis (*The Garden of Eichstätt*), first published in 1613, has been described as the greatest botanical picture book ever created. Certainly it was one of the biggest. An enormous thing, measuring two feet by a foot and a half and containing some 367 plates depicting more than a thousand different plants, it was bound in two volumes so large that, according to one commentator, they had to be moved in a wheelbarrow. Sir Thomas Browne called the book the most "massive" of herbals. It was also without question one of the loveliest, especially the hand-colored copies. These cost a staggering five hundred florins, at a time when a head gardener could be hired for sixty florins a year.

Thanks to an exceptional piece of modern bookmaking, we can get a sense of this beauty at a somewhat more reasonable price. Under the auspices of the British Library, the bibliographical scholar Nicholas Barker has published, in large folio size, a study of the book with many pages in reproduction and a fascinating text. Browsing through it, I couldn't help being struck not only by the technical excellence of the plant illustrations, but also by the evident freshness, sometimes even amounting to surprise, with which the artists viewed the plants themselves. It was as if these unique living objects were being examined carefully for the first time. Of course, in some cases—newly bred tulip crosses, for example, or the enormous *Agave americana*—they really were.

The original publisher of *Hortus Eystettensis* was a botanist–apothecary of Nuremberg named Basileus Besler. It was Besler who oversaw the teams of painters, engravers, and colorists, and Besler who found the buyers, mostly minor princes and rich burghers building libraries and collecting plants of their own. Behind the book, however, was a garden, and a gardener, by all odds a most unusual gardener.

Johann Conrad von Gemmingen became Bishop of Eichstätt, a small diocese halfway between Munich and Nuremberg, in 1595, when he was thirty-four. He was already rich, and was to get richer through family inheritances. He was also well educated, and had traveled in Italy, France, and England, cultivating, in the words of one acquaintance, "a policy of few words, open ears and an open mind, journeying not as spiders but as bees." There is an unconfirmed story that as a young man in England he served as a page to Elizabeth I.

The bishop's palace perched atop a steep hill called the Willibaldsburg overlooking the river Altmuhl and the town of Eichstätt. Not the easiest place to build a garden, perhaps, but that hardly deterred Johann Conrad. Amidst his many official duties—he was apparently tough on witches, but liberal in his relations with Jews, relaxing various prohibitions—he set about designing a complicated and expensive new layout for the palace and its grounds. The basic aim was to create spaces and suitable environments to grow a vast variety of plants—not only vegetables, fruit, and medicinal herbs, but also plants distinguished purely by their beauty or rarity. This was something new.

The second half of the sixteenth century was an exciting and expansive time in plantsmanship. "Never before or since," says historian W. T. Stearn, "has there been such an astonishing influx of colorful strange plants," largely from Turkey and the Near East—lilies, tulips, irises, anemones, fritillaries. More were coming from the Americas. And with this abundance there was increasing interest in growing flowers and developing new cultivars. In his *De Historia Stirpium* (1542), Leonhard Fuchs listed only about five hundred plants; by 1623, Caspar Bauhin could describe more than six thousand. For a sophisticated nobleman like the Bishop of Eichstätt, moved not only by an interest in science and the collection of rarities, but also by a theological impulse to understand and celebrate God's grace in creating the natural world, botany was a logical predilection.

Four hundred years on, in the wake of countless wars and many generations of plant life, we would be unlikely to have any firsthand impression of the bishop's garden except for a lucky accident. In March 1611, a much-traveled art dealer from Augsburg named Philipp Hainhofer arrived on a semi-diplomatic visit. He was a sort of royal go-between, an agent acting as a scout, a collector, and information-gatherer, and his call on the Bishop of Eichstätt involved making inquiries on behalf of one of his princely patrons. Fortuitously, Hainhofer's visit came at a time when the bishop's garden-making was in full swing, and work on the great florilegium had already begun.

As the bishop himself was indisposed when Hainhofer arrived (he was actually very ill "from a congestion in the lungs," and would die the next year), his steward and chamberlain escorted the visitor around the episcopal palace. There were, according to Hainhofer's account, eight different gardens, each containing plants from a different country, varying in the style of the beds and the flowers, "especially the beautiful roses, lilies, tulips, among other flowers." The gardens were "partly adorned with painted walls and pleasure rooms," and apparently linked by pavilions. Each garden had its own gardener in charge, and "none infringes on the other's domain."

The next day, Hainhofer passed through glassed galleries outside the bishop's rooms filled with plants—pansies ("red, yellow, brown, and speckled") in flowerpots, and tubs of violets, apricots, pomegranates, lemons, and the enamel-leafed *Amaranthus tricolor*. These could apparently be moved outdoors during the summer and then into the heated galleries for the cold weather. Outside, on the balconies, six large blocks of wood served as bases to support as many dead trees where in the winter singing birds would come and be fed while entertaining the bishop. Other fragments of information suggest that he had accumulated many extremely costly varieties of plants, including, by his own boast, "tulips in five hundred colors, almost all different."

Where did the plants for what the bishop improbably called his "modest, narrow little garden" come from? In a letter to Hainhofer's patron, he explained that he had secured them "through the offices of local merchants" from the Netherlands, "for example from Antwerp, Brussels, Amsterdam and other places." These were, of course, the principal transshipment points for rare plants from all over the world at the time, especially from Turkey and the Near East (narcissi and hyacinths, and of course tulips), but also such plants as sunflowers, nicotianas, evening primroses, Michaelmas daisies, and so on from the New World. And with the unprecedented new taste for flowers, even native German weeds were being crossbred or introduced in their original forms for garden use.

It is clear from his comprehensive interest in collecting and growing unusual plants that the Bishop of Eichstätt was a true plantsman, but we have far stronger proof. It lies in the grand book named after his garden and illustrating its contents (and other plants), the *Hortus Eystettensis*. Hainhofer notes that at the time of his visit, the bishop's "most precious drawings," the plant pictures he had been commissioning from a range of artists, were not in the palace but had been sent to Basileus Besler in Nuremberg to be used in the preparation of a book that he intended to publish. In addition, "one or two boxes full of fresh flowers" were being dispatched to Besler each week to be sketched.

Unfortunately, the bishop did not live to see his book completed. Besler took over, financing the project and eventually publishing the huge volumes successfully; reprints from the original plates continued to appear for more than two hundred years. *Hortus Eystettensis* remains a landmark not only in botany but in art, an extraordinary expression of the painter and engraver's skill. Even more, perhaps, it is a record of the beauty of the plants themselves, a testament to the plantsman's ethic. The colored copies—Barker estimates that between twenty and thirty survive—are treasured and literally priceless rarities.

Judging from Hainhofer's description of the amount of building work still going on only shortly before the bishop's death, we may assume that the garden, like the book, was far from finished. (What garden ever is?) The new bishop kept it up to a degree, although not on quite the same plan; along with much of Central Europe in the 1630s, the palace on the mountain was ravaged in the Thirty Years War. In the early eighteenth century, yet another bishop "improved" the garden, laying out paths, shrubs, and trees. After that, it fell into disuse, to the point where there was scarcely a garden to be seen. At the start of the nineteenth century, a local official lamented that it was now impossible to make out its location. Explorations of the ruins atop the Willibaldsburg revealed just four living reminders of the fact that a great plantsman had once gardened here: a snapdragon, a garden violet, honeysuckle, and a yellow horned poppy.

REGINALD FARRER'S LAST JOURNEY

✣

In one of his final letters, to his cousin and boyhood friend Osbert Sitwell, Reginald Farrer described his situation:

> *Right away over on the far side of the uttermost edge of nowhere, I sit in a little bamboo shanty, open at every pore to all the winds that blow, surrounded, far overhead, by inky black peaks like flames in a tempest, frozen suddenly . . . So now I'm happy as the day is long, working hard among the plants, and camping on high passes, full of snow and midges . . .*

The year was 1920, the place Upper Burma, in the midst of virtually unexplored mountains on the Chinese frontier. Reginald Farrer was forty, author of half a dozen novels—mostly unreadable—and twice as many irresistibly prolix, colorful, inspiring, opinionated, influential books on plants, plant-hunting, and rock gardens. In a few weeks, he would be dead.

The annals of plant collecting are full of odd characters, but it would be difficult to find one who combined quite as many oddities as Reginald Farrer. He was born the scion of a wealthy Yorkshire family and grew to be a handsome (if slightly bulky) man, blighted by a harelip that neither painful surgery nor a large moustache could wholly mask. His voice was high-pitched. Sitwell found it "as startling as the discordant cry of a jay or woodpecker." But his mind moved with huge agility, and he was never, ever, at a loss for words.

From childhood, Farrer was a loner. He loved wandering across the high limestone fells near his home, finding and puzzling over alpine plants. When he was only fourteen, the *Journal of Botany* noted his discovery of a rare *Arenaria*, and a few years later he found an unrecorded hybrid saxifrage, the first of many plants to bear his name. He started his own rock garden, and at Oxford helped a fellow alpine enthusiast construct a sizeable alpine garden at St. John's College, all the time gaining increasingly detailed knowledge of the horticultural demands of plants from high places. It apparently never occurred to him, however, to engage in any formal botanical study.

Farrer decided soon after leaving Oxford to be a traveler and a writer. His first long journey took him to China and Japan and yielded a book called *The Garden of Asia: Impressions from Japan* (1904). Like his later books, it rejoiced in sharp descriptive phrases that often drifted into pure purple, and displayed a truly exceptional ability to talk about individual plants in memorable terms. Not all of his readers appreciated this. One obituarist later observed that "he wrote vividly, often at the top of his voice, as it were . . . he always had something to say." What is amazing is that so much of what he said remains highly original and engaging.

Tossing off a couple of novels in the interim, in 1907 Farrer published the first—and most reprinted—of his gardening books, *My Rock Garden*. It is a blend of how-to and sharply expressed opinion, largely in support of his own plantsman's approach, in which the rock structure should come second to the cultural demands of the alpines. This position was to be elaborated later in his magnum opus, the vast two-volume compendium of rock plant description and celebration, *The English Rock Garden* (1919). Never one for tact, Farrer managed to anger a number of contemporaries with skillful attacks on *their* rock gardens ("bald and chaotic barrenness"), while reviewers occasionally balked ("We have seldom met with a work wherein the author's self-satisfaction was so conspicuous").

Around 1907, influenced by his oriental travels (or possibly his instinctive wish to be different), he turned Buddhist and made a trip to Ceylon to visit shrines. Subsequent journeys, often to the Alps and frequently in company with fellow gardener Edward Augustus Bowles, were for the more worldly purpose of collecting plants. Farrer was a great believer in plant collecting, convinced that even the rarer species would never suffer extinction. "If all the collectors in all the world with all their sacks, combined to toil at the task for months and years, I do not believe they could strip even one range of the Alps of their *Eritricium*," he wrote in *Among the Hills*, a delightful account of clamberings in the Swiss, French, and Italian Alps. (Such an attitude would doubtless be frowned upon today, but the fact is that the gemlike blue *Eritricium nanum* is a good deal easier to collect than to propagate.)

Much as Farrer enjoyed his Alpine jaunts, the idea of actually finding new and unknown species lured him to wilder territories. Not just any species, of course, but plants that would be both hardy in the British climate and worthwhile for gardeners to grow. (Farrer disdained "weeds," even weeds that nobody had ever seen before.) Hard terrain held no terrors for him. "He would walk," a friend observed, "with an odd little swagger, perfect grace, fearless poise, even in the worst places, and quite tirelessly . . ."

His first target, reached just before the outbreak of World War I, was the mountains of Northwest Kansu Province in China, where he went with the experienced plant hunter William Purdum. The expedition was a success, at least to the extent that Farrer and Purdum emerged alive in spite of the unsettled political conditions, brigands, and warlike monks, and Farrer got a couple of books out of it (*On the Eaves of the World* and *The Rainbow Bridge*). But the war meant that relatively few of the plants they introduced survived into cultivation. Among those that did were *Geranium farreri*, *Gentiana farreri*, and *Buddleia davidii* var. *nanhoensis*.

Returning to wartime England in 1915, Farrer worked in the Ministry of Information, wrote, and corrected *The English Rock Garden*. No sooner did hostilities end, however, than he was off again to the Far East. This time, choosing a search area was much more difficult. Plant hunters better known (and funded) than Farrer were already at work in the choicest spots—E. H. "Chinese" Wilson in Hupei and Szechuan; George Forrest in Yunnan; and Frank Kingdon-Ward all over the place, from Tibet to Burma. Nor would any old region do. The locale had to be remote and rich in unfamiliar plants, and also—especially in South Asia—high enough to encourage the sort of hardiness capable of surviving European winters. Plant hunting was, after all, a business. Commercial nurserymen, botanical gardens, and syndicates of rich amateurs put up the money and in return expected beautiful objects they could sell or grow.

What was left for Farrer and his companion, E. M. H. Cox, was the peculiarly inhospitable range of high mountains running north-south along the edge of Burma, just west of the long gorge of the Salween River. This was not totally virgin territory, but so dense with vegetation that a great deal remained to be found. As Cox put it later, in a book about the venture, "The truth is that the whole country is overgrown: it is nothing more than a giant propagating bed." Much of the landscape was either jungle or—above ten thousand feet—smothered in an endless blanket of scrub bamboo and rhododendron. Yet some of the rhododendrons were new, while higher up a wide variety of alpines grew amid the screes and pocket meadows.

During the first season, Cox kept Farrer company, working out of a government post in the village of Hpimaw. Living conditions were acceptable—the police bungalow where they stayed at least shed the incessant rain—but there were other drawbacks: bamboo ticks "the size of young crabs," snakes (when Farrer stepped on a ball of newly hatched snakelets, Cox notes, "it was the only time I have seen him flustered"), blister flies, the boredom of waiting for the weather to clear so that they could explore the high passes. In collecting terms, the summer was a fair success—a large number of rhododendrons (although nothing to compare with Forrest's finds, and few that reached cultivation back home), gentians, primulas (including the fabled *P. agleniana*, subsequently lost), *Nomocharis pardanthina*, and possibly best of all, Cox's Chinese coffin tree, *Juniperus recurva* var. *coxii*.

That winter, after the seed harvest, Cox went back to England, and Farrer stayed on, determined to go still further north in spring. This time he traveled alone, accompanied only by his Gurkha majordomo Bhaju and some bearers, into an extremely difficult region near the point where Burma, India, and China come together. Regular reports to the *Gardener's Chronicle* in London described his adventures in getting there, and the near impossibility of working in one of the world's most sodden places. On the Shing Hong Pass, after a hard four-day walk: "For now I have lived for ten days in an unvarying fog of soaking rain . . . It was all deadness, lit by the pale glare of the drenching fog." On the Chawchi Pass in July: "I took my camp to 12,000 feet and affixed it, like a temple-haunting martlet's nest, to some rocks below the pass . . . for the whole of my three weeks up there it never ceased to pour with rain but once for an hour." Yet the plant hunter's dream kept him going: "To these delights, too, are invariably added those of always feeling that there must be a sky-blue rhododendron or a pea-green primula somewhere just out of sight, in the unfathomable white gloom."

So far as we know—none of his seeds and few of his herbarium specimens from that last season ever reached Britain—Farrer never found his sky-blue rhododendron. His reports to the *Chronicle* and the letters he wrote to friends speak of many other wonders: a "citron-colored" frit-illary, "a *Meconopsis* of the integrifolia persuasion," *Rhododendron aperantum* ("It is simply one of the most radi-antly lovely things you ever saw"), "an unspotted Nomo-charis with flowers of a tone unknown to me in all hardy Liliaceae, of a pure salmon flame-colour," and dozens more, described with inexhaustible (perhaps one should say undampened) enthusiasm. As had happened before, some of them would doubtlessly have turned out to be already known; Farrer's lack of formal botanical training sometimes tripped him up. But no botanist ever loved plants better than he did or discussed them with greater joy.

As autumn 1920 drew on, he ended his last dispatch to the *Chronicle* by noting that exploration was nearly over and "nothing will be left to do but rest and gather strength again, against the final whirlwind of the harvest." He was already making new plans—for a trip to Nepal and Tibet on the one hand, and on the other to get married (he asked his college friend Aubrey Herbert to help find him a wife). But the harvest never came. On October 1, huddling for cover in his bamboo shanty surrounded by specimens that he was trying to dry before shipment, Farrer fell ill. Little more than two weeks later he died, in spite of Bhaju's valiant but fruitless attempt to get help from the nearest fort, five or six days and a flooded river away. The official cause was diphtheria, although Cox doubted it, considering the remoteness of the place and the fact that it was virtually uninhabited.

When it was all over, as he reported in a letter to Cox, Bhaju saw to it that Farrer was buried "with as very careful as much as I can," and then supervised the packing of what he regarded as Farrer's most valuable effects—the tents, the remaining tinned goods and other supplies, his frying pan and his boots, "all the furnitures of my master." Less important things had to be left behind: "there were many kinds of flowers and seeds there . . . and we could not bring them off."

A great many plants bear Reginald Farrer's name today; W. T. Stearn lists no fewer than twenty-nine, ranging from *Allium cyathophorum* var. *farreri* to *Viburnum farreri*. Yet on the whole, his talents as a plant hunter could not compare with men like Forrest or Wilson, nor was he a great gardener in an age of great gardeners. What made him memorable—and still does—was his enthusiasm. If it occasionally led him into excess (he could describe a modest little *Omphalogramma*, for example, in terms to make an ad man blush*), it nevertheless brought into the world of horticulture a rare and lasting kind of excitement. We need that as much as we need a blue rhododendron.

---

*"Nor does it lag in beauty . . . here the emarginate turned-back lobes are in sixes or sevens, narrow, more or less entire, broadening to the cleft at their end, and the colour is superb, being really less of a violet blue than of real sapphire, or very dark, cornflower one . . . Like stars of blue velvet midnight," etc., etc.

IV

SHOWS AND

SHOWPLACES

THE HAMPTON COURT PALACE
FLOWER SHOW

❧

Hampton Court, the royal palace on the edge of London, has been a place to go to look at gardens for quite a while—four hundred years, roughly. Henry VIII, while he wasn't otherwise occupied, had a splendid spread there. King William, newly arrived from Holland in 1688, spent a fortune building a private garden in the best Dutch style (which, newly restored, is now open to the public). Today we've got the Hampton Court Palace Flower Show, billed as the largest in Britain, which of course means the largest in the world. Apart from the invasion of plebs, Henry and William would no doubt be pleased and gratified.

"The thing is, it's just so vaaast!"

There is no obvious significance in the fact that this year the Hampton Court Show opened on the Fourth of July. Possibly the most revolutionary thing about the day was the weather—blazing sun, hard on the heels of about three weeks of uninterrupted sun, weather one might more likely expect to find in the purlieus of Kansas City than London. Yet the English take this in stride, aided by the thoughtfulness of their merchant class: on the very grounds of the flower show you could buy not only a wheelbarrow, a lawn-mower, or a good-sized £8 frangipani, but a hat. A fine panama cost £15, but the cricket hat I chose was only £5 and good for years of hot work in the garden or on the pitch.

In retrospect, I'm very glad I bought that hat. It saved me from sunstroke and let me blend with the crowd. And in this role of American interloper, bemused amid the hallucinatory abundance of flowers, terra-cotta pots, wrought-iron weathervanes, wickerwork settees, patent compost makers, and painted wooden signs saying GONE TO PUB and BEWARE THE GOOSE, and above all listening to the comments of the gardeners around me, I began to sense as never before the degree to which British gardening is a national obsession.

". . . and you bring it in over the winter."
"Oh God."
"That put you off?"

Everyone's heard of Chelsea, but Hampton Court has charms that the older event cannot match. For one thing, it's bigger—800 exhibitors as against 440 for Chelsea, covering 25 acres to Chelsea's eight. More important than that, in the view of practicing gardeners as opposed to those who might be called garden tourists, just about everything at Hampton Court is for sale from the start. At Chelsea you have to wait until the last day, at which time there is a maddened rush to snag choice plants before they collapse from over-admiration.

"That tree's got nothing to do."

Hampton Court would of course hardly be a flower show without the classic, staggeringly labor-intensive displays—perfect streptocarpus in the thousands covering what looks like a mountainside, and more fuchsias, in more different colors, than I had ever imagined seeing in one place (unless in a nightmare). Many visitors come simply to gape. But most of the exhibitors here—upward of 160 specialist growers from all over the country (including a few from the Continent)—bring along with them a large quantity of potted pret-a-porter stock. So if you can't stand going home empty handed, there's an opportunity to buy a few pots of whatever strikes you as irresistible. Of course, changing fashions and the number of true buffs roaming the aisles means that you may have to move smartly. I was buying a small *Origanum vulgare* 'Aureum' from a stand run by the holder of the National Origanum Collection when I noticed that every other customer was asking for 'Beauty of Kent' and being told that it had sold out on the first day. I hunted around and found it in the display. I'd call it only mildly interesting, but then I wanted *my* oregano to eat.

To make it even easier to buy plants, the show had a créche (the British term for a day nursery for little kids) with special couriers on hand to transport your purchases for later pickup. Given the crowds (and on this day the heat), it was a great idea.

"Wow. Good, innit?"

And crowds there were. Official figures issued following the show put the number of visitors at 210,000. This works out to some forty thousand a day, most of whom appeared to be standing in front of me at any one time. I wouldn't even venture to guess how many plants, but you can be sure that in the whole place there was not one square inch of Astroturf. You walked on grass (or on wood chips where feet had worn the grass thin), and whenever a design called for greenery, even on a vertical surface, only the real thing would do. An example of this, which I'd prefer not to think about just now, was a bizarre "folly" misguidedly based on *Alice in Wonderland*, incorporating mirrors, large playing cards, and grass-covered walls curving perilously overhead.

"That's nice. You've got that one, haven't you?"

One of the first things you see, crossing one of the special pontoon bridges over Hampton Court Palace's Long Water, is a full-sized thatched cottage under one end of a huge tent. This is a crucial fantasy: in fact, it may be the central fantasy behind the whole phenomenon of the British love of gardening. In this case, the fantasy is explicit. The *Daily Mail* newspaper, one of the main sponsors of the flower show, had not only bought and refurbished an actual Nineteenth-Century Dream Cottage in the Hampshire countryside on the edge of the New Forest, complete with "a beautifully designed one acre garden," to be given away in a draw, it constructed a plausible full-sized mock-up of the cottage right here at Hampton Court—thatch, tape-recorded birdsong, and all. It could have been abstracted from Disneyland, except for one thing: the plantings around it were meticulous and real. Apparently growing in rich dark soil was a collection of cottagey flowers and shrubs that included everything from *Alchemilla mollis* to golden sage to sweet peas clambering up peasticks. Wildflowers, too—corn marigold, spiked speedwell, red campion. And if it didn't run to an acre, the garden was still breathtaking. You could almost believe it, apart from the fact that everything was blooming simultaneously. They don't do that in *my* cottage garden.

"The best thing is, put 'em in a pot. Put 'em in a pot."

Credit for devising one of the most ingenious (and, I suppose, expensive) displays must go to the department store chain Marks and Spencer, which constructed a lifesize replica of considerable parts of the old Covent Garden fruit and vegetable market, filling it with an array of, well, fruit and vegetables. There were also flowers—cut peonies and bundles of carnations, tulips and roses—and, as an especially nice touch, an old-fashioned tea stand equipped with dirty cups, a set mousetrap, half-eaten buns, and a sign saying "Please do not throw slops on the ground." Nostalgia is an English vice: it's been twenty years since you could buy a cabbage in the real Covent Garden.

"That's what's coming up all over the place, of course."

The overall size of the Hampton Court show makes it hard to come to grips with. Seemingly endless booths pushing objects that may be described politely as peripheral to gardening (handmade chocolates, leatherwork, old-fashioned twig brooms) jostled marketers of garden tools, worm composters, pesticides, and irrigation systems. You want a pergola? Step this way. How about an urn? We've got them made of lead, ceramic, or an absolutely amazing plastic that looks like all the other stuff, but older. As for the plants, which are after all the heart of the matter, you don't have to be an expert to enjoy yourself thoroughly—I can testify to that—but if you *are* an expert (and a good many of the locals certainly seemed to be), the huge marquees comprising the focus of the show contained limitless horticultural delicacies.

"The only thing is, the leaves get a bit big."

I was fortunate in visiting Hampton Court with an expert

friend, who filled me in as we went along. Not that we noticed everything, or even a fraction of the available wonders. But I now know that I would like *Dierama pulcherrimum* nodding among the flagstones, a fine blue-gray *Hosta* 'Halcyon' clustering in a particular damp spot, and a few of the tall, thin *Verbena bonariensis* 'Patagonia' screening one end of the perennial bed. We spotted a delightful little hebe called 'Mist Maiden' bearing tiny light-blue flowers and *Verbascum chaixii* 'Gainsborough', a jolly spiring yellow that everybody except me probably already has. I'm less inclined to try the cosmos that smells like chocolate (although I now know that it really does), or a *Physostegia* (obedient plant) despite its cooperative habit, or the *Sisyrinchium* only one centimeter in diameter. Nice to know such things exist, though.

"We've done that one. How do we get out?"

Then there were the really big specialist displays. Clematis, for example. The British climate is generally kind to clematis, and with the new fashion of letting them wander everywhere, over hedges and into trees and through your mahonia, they are increasingly popular. A grower called Valley Clematis managed to put together a sensational display of clematis varieties climbing four or five twenty-foot trelliswork towers, all blooming vigorously and looking as though they had been there the whole summer. There must have been forty kinds—and all for sale in pots too. I cannot imagine how such perfection was achieved, although my friend advises that the trick is to grow roughly four times as many plants as will be needed and then behave ruthlessly.

"No, the man said water. Water."

In some ways a big English flower show like Chelsea or Hampton Court is like a debutante party, and big growers make a point of introducing their most glamorous new offspring. We were presented with a couple of new pelargoniums ('Debbie': "in a decorative burgundy and pale pink, its petals have an attractive crinkly edge"; and 'Barnston Dale', a deep purple double), while Norfolk Lavender came up with four new varieties. Bressingham Gardens, whose speciality is perennials, offered one that to my eye looks as odd as its name—*Eryngium* 'Jos Eisjking', a blue thistle with stems that are also robin's-egg blue, or, if you prefer, the blue (and general appearance) of blue plastic cable. Striking, if you like to be struck. I felt much more drawn to the sweet peas which, if not new introductions, were largely new to me. Early July in England being sweet-pea season, they turned up all over the show in plantings and displays. At least two specialist growers—Diane Sewell and S. & N. Brackley—had nothing but sweet peas, arranged in vast bunches in rising ranks of color. I am unable to explain why, but most of the varieties seemed to be named after relatively elderly television stars. This hardly slowed business in the seeds at about a dollar for a packet of fifteen.

"This gets worse and worse. Isn't that lovely?"

The Hampton Court show began in a small way only six years ago. Three years ago it was taken over by the Royal Horticultural Society and promoted—with great efficiency—as a counterpart to Chelsea. Because it has more room than the older show, it can accommodate more of everything—more stalls, more visitors (including more parking, a mixed blessing given the neighborhood's eighteenth-century-sized jam-prone roads), and more show gardens constructed around the margins of the show ground. There were twenty-five of these show gardens, ranging from a Caribbean spread featuring bougainvillea, hibiscus, and sugar cane (plus a sandy beach with shipwreck) to a biblical garden designed by the Bleasdale Church of England Primary School. The intent was to offer "snappy design ideas." While I wouldn't go as far as Robin Lane Fox, who dismissed them all in the *Financial Times* as "ghastly" (he was getting over a traffic jam), they might well confound anyone convinced that English gardening taste is infallible.

"Topiary? Easy. Just keep chopping."

The Hampton Court Palace Flower Show goes on for five days, six if you count the fairly crowded first day limited to RHS members. I suspect that you could go every day and still be finding new things at the end. The last thing I found was John Ainsworth's unsettling display of meat-eating *Sarracenia* or pitcher plants, billed as the largest collection ever seen in Britain. It may well be; I shan't search for a larger. After looking at it, I needed a sandwich. I'm happy to report that Hampton Court has a fine line in sandwiches, fish and chips, spit-roasted chicken, draft beer, champagne cocktails, baked potatoes, ice cream cones . . .

COURSON

❧

Living in England, surrounded by some of the best gardens—and gardeners—in the world, it is sometimes difficult to remember that this is not the only place in Europe with horticulture to boast about. To your average chauvinist Englishman, Holland, in spite of all those tulips and hyacinths, is just too flat; Italy and Spain too sunbaked; and France—well, France is too French, meaning too affected, either with Le Nôtrean grandiosity or (more recently) with the kind of finicking ugliness (gravel, wrought iron, and pampas grass) Jacques Tati took off so savagely in his film *Mon Oncle*. Okay, Monet made a garden at Giverny and painted it so often that people started thinking it exceptional. But when you come right down to it, Giverny's not a lot more than a Japanese bridge and a half dozen cutting beds.

Mea culpa. The English may indeed be better at this particular activity than most people, but a visit to a chateau a few miles south of Paris has forced me to recognize that French gardeners know what they are doing too, and what they are doing can be spectacular.

The occasion was the autumn flower show, the *Journées des Plantes*, which is held twice a year at the Chateau de Courson. Courson is a sort of intimate Chelsea, smaller and less hectic, with the displays spread out over several acres of parkland near the chateau itself. The brainchild of Patrice Fustier and his wife Hélène (the chateau has been in Hélène's family for centuries), the show has been going on for only twelve years. Yet this fall, more than two hundred exhibitors showed up with everything from lithiops to fifteen-foot oak trees, and roughly twenty thousand garden buffs turned out to admire, criticize, buy, and proudly carry away.

Chateau de Courson is located in a hilly farming region laced by motorways and dotted with industrial parks and housing developments only twenty or thirty miles from Paris. Three hundred years ago, when the chateau was built (parts of it are much older), the area was apparently regarded as choice, a Gallic Westchester or Main Line; a number of other chateaux are in the immediate neighborhood, and Versailles is not far away. Courson is especially fortunate in retaining most of its surrounding land, some seventy acres, including a vast park as beautifully planted and graceful in its maturity as anything conceived by Lancelot "Capability" Brown—lake, huge oaks and ashes and cedars, columnar evergreens black against old chestnuts, roughly mowed lawns stretching away into the misty distance. Very English, in fact.

The morning I arrived, the mist was not distant at all, but all around us, soft and white. There was still a bustle of exhibitors carrying baskets of plants for last-minute setups, while others busied themselves pulling tarpaulins off displays of potted orange trees and box topiary. I paused at the entrance to ask for M. Fustier, who soon clattered up aboard a golf cart to welcome me. (Since an accident some years ago, he has had to contend with a gimpy leg, so the golf cart was a practical necessity.) Dapper, dressed *à la Anglaise* in flannels and a double-breasted blue blazer, he spoke flawless and warmly cordial English.

Unlike the Royal Horticultural Society's Chelsea or Hampton Court shows, Courson is a purely private enterprise, one which grew out of the Fustiers's own new-found obsession with plants and gardening. In 1980, after several years of contemplating the decay of the chateau's glorious early-nineteenth-century park (described in the brochure, with perfect accuracy, as a "somptueux parc romantique") beneath weeds and sycamore seedlings, the family had begun its restoration. At first they knew little, but they engaged the help of a young English landscape designer named Timothy Vaughan (whose own garden in northern Brittany is now a showpiece) and started learning. One thing they soon learned was that the particular trees they needed were simply not available from major French nurseries, but only in England and Holland.

Then, in 1982, a lucky coincidence brought a group of French botanical garden owners to Courson to view the Fustiers's progress and exchange plants. One visitor, and then two others, asked if it would be all right to sell plants instead. Fustier agreed and thus, very modestly, on a Saturday afternoon in October, the Courson show was born. An unexpected bonus was Fustier's discovery that he could get the trees he wanted in France after all. It had simply been a matter of finding the right growers, smaller ones, and encouraging them.

Today, instead of three exhibitors, Courson has hundreds, primarily French but also many from abroad. (This year there were fifteen from England, with Belgium, Germany, Italy, and even China represented.) Unlike Chelsea or Hampton Court, it has no show gardens, only stands for exhibits. Yet the range of plants on display, and frequently their rarity, is such as to make even Chelsea look just a little bumpkinlike.

This impression was reinforced for me by the apparent sophistication of the visitors strolling across the lawns of Courson on the opening morning. By tradition, this time is reserved for professionals, the press, and—especially—invited guests. Watching them examine the stock while exhibitors busily put finishing touches on the displays—rearranging pots, syringing drooping foliage, tying up the last wayward stems of clematis—it soon became clear that gardening is a serious business in France and one that particularly appeals to the wealthy. Not that the plant prices were out of line—although $100 for a *Paeonia suffruticosa* ssp. *rockii* (see p. 00) struck me as steep—but the buying going on was unbridled. One extremely elegant gentleman in pinstripes appeared to be furnishing an entire park in rare oaks and maples, while another did his best to acquire the whole stock—about thirty plants—of a Himalayan gentian, *Gentiana* 'Barbara Lyle' ("très, très rare") from John Ward, an English grower, at sixty francs ($12.60) each. (Ward, who can propagate only eighty plants a year at most, let him have ten.)

To be fair, it ought to be said that this first-morning crowd was not wholly typical; the hoi polloi began arriving in the afternoon. But even then you could not help seeing the social linkages between gardening, fashion, and—oddly enough—England here in France. Far from disdaining the *rosbifs*, the true BCBG* Frenchman or woman seems determined to emulate them, no matter what the cost. From the Wellington boots so much in evidence to the amount of English being spoken to the tables stacked with imported

---

*BCBG stands for *bon chic bon genre*, a phrase coined some years ago to refer to wealthy and well-born young trendsetters; they are older now and even wealthier.

Aran fisherman's sweaters and Barbour jackets in the Country Store [sic], I occasionally got the uneasy feeling that I was not in France at all, but back in Blighty.

Certainly the variety of the plants and the quality of the plantsmanship was comparable to anything I've seen in England. At each Courson show, a panel of distinguished judges gives awards of merit to plants in nine categories, from trees to "plantes de serre et d'orangerie," based on botanical interest, ornamental quality, and rarity, plants that deserve to be better known and more readily available. Over the years, these awards have called attention to such prizes as the orchid *Dactylorhiza elata*, *Cornus kousa* 'Satomi' (a fine hardy dogwood), *Phyllostachys aurea* 'Koi' (a golden bamboo "pour des grands espaces"), and dozens of others, from camellias to *Schizophragma hydrangeoides*. This year, winners included two interesting ornamental grasses, *Miscanthus sinensis* 'Kleine Fontäne' and *M. sinensis* 'Morning Light', as well as an American native that probably looks more exotic in Dijon than in Detroit—*Eupatorium coelestinum*, a hardy relative of the well-known ageratum.

Apart from the prize plants, there were splendid finds for the browser. Plenty of clematises still in rich bloom, no doubt as confused by the abnormally warm fall as their English brethren. I noted a handsome *Hydrangea quercifolia* 'Snow Queen' dressed in its deep red autumn foliage, and there were lots of asters—dozens of kinds of *A. novi belgii*—including a few New England asters that I would have said were weeds. Autumn-flowering bulbs in abundance—colchicums, cyclamens—and a fine array of trees ranging from the rare (*Gelsemium sempervirens* 'Pride of Augusta') to oaks and birches and an entire National Collection of liquidambars. One exhibit could have been nowhere but in France: in the converted stables housing several rare book dealers and a grower of orchids, Jean-F. Laporte, Maître Parfumeur et Gantier (glover), had set up two or three big round stone-topped tables bearing little pots of floral essence. Anyone feeling the need for a spot of aromatherapy was invited to have a free sniff.

As the morning wore on, the fog began to thin and lift, and I began to get an even stronger sense of the beauty of Courson's setting. Many of the exhibits were sheltered under giant horse chestnuts in the park, which now stopped dripping. (The hundreds of nuts underfoot were a strong reminder that we were not in England; there, I suspect, they would have been gathered by schoolboys keen to play conkers.) Other displays backed onto the chateau's own plantings, sometimes disconcertingly—the stems and feathery foliage on sale by the charmingly named La Bambouseraie, for example, seemed to be growing inexplicably right into a giant bank of M. Fustier's viburnum.

While it would be irresponsible to attempt to say anything very profound about French gardens on the strength of a visit to one flower show, it is obvious that a great fund of horticultural sophistication and interest exists there. The blending of French formality and English romance in garden design has been going on for a long time now—two hundred years at least. It has already borne remarkable fruit and will no doubt bear much more. I coincidentally had proof of this at Courson, although not, I regret to say, directly. M. Fustier invited me to a buffet lunch being given on the lawn outside one of the show's several restaurants in honor of the publication of a new book about a French garden. Kerdalo, rightly described as one of the major gardens of the twentieth century, was created in a remote part of Brittany over a period of twenty-five years by Peter Wolkonsky, who is now a hale ninety-four. Happily, he was able to come to the launch party (wearing, I was pleased to see, his battered English tweed gardening cap) and receive the congratulations of the guests. Judging from pictures in the book, Kerdalo is as pretty and *romantique* as anything in England, yet it also has the "bones" of its French heritage in its box hedging and stonework. I'd love to see it. So far as *Le jardin Français* is concerned, I'm a convert.

A DOME AWAY FROM HOME

❧

I t's possible that Kew once looked like this, but I find it hard to imagine.

We are standing on a creosoted timber platform on the crest of a low hill in deepest Wales. The day is overcast, a sullen, typically gray, early-winter day in this part of the world, about as depressing as any weather can be. But the view is anything but depressing: a splendid 360-degree sweep from north to south and round again, over shallow valleys filled with second-growth trees, across grazed fields squared up with hedges, up to ridges capped with bigger trees and even an impressive stone tower, black against the sky. A couple of small farmsteads lurk in sheltered declivities. This is the estate of Middleton, its 568 acres including pretty much everything you can see, the site of what is destined to be Britain's newest, biggest, and most impressive botanic garden: the National Botanic Garden of Wales.

William Wilkins, the man behind this enterprise, is a vigorous, fine-drawn, clear-spoken fellow in his fifties who has so far raised more than £33 million ($54.8 million) toward paying for it, with about £10 million still to go. He has done this not as a botanist or scientist or administrator or professional fund-raiser, but as, you might say, an amateur—an amateur in the honorable eighteenth-century sense of the term. Wilkins is in fact an artist, a painter, and, incidentally, a gardener. "I have never pretended to have the skills of the sort required to set this thing up," he says. "But nobody has." To him, the botanic garden is basically a dream, which—helped along by serendipity and the joined enthusiasms of dozens of others—has blossomed into grand and unexpected reality. You get the feeling that he still doesn't quite believe it.

Standing on the spot where Middleton Hall itself once commanded the splendors of its parks and plantings (the house burned to the ground in 1931), Wilkins describes—with all the excitement of a boy with a new toy—what has happened here in the past and what is very soon going to happen in the future. Both aspects of the project are important. As he puts it, the aim is to marry the aesthetic achievement of the eighteenth century with the scientific ambitions of the twentieth—and twenty-first.

The fact is, of course, that except for the lay of the land, there is not a great deal left of the original Middleton. The chain of lakes arcing below us are simply marshy hollows mostly choked with brush; the old trees that should be making dramatic clumps and accent points are gone, long since cut down for timber. The vast double-walled Italian garden—unique in Britain—is weed filled and beginning to crumble. Complicated water features, the cascades and artificial waterfalls and dams, are either vanished, dried up, or—what may be worse—clumsily restored by municipal workers who kept no record of original levels or sluiceways.

Originally responsible for all this was an immensely rich nabob named Sir William Paxton, who bought Middleton upon his return from India in 1786. Having failed to get himself elected to Parliament in spite of keeping the voters of Llandeilo drunk for a week on 25,000 gallons of free beer, 11,000 bottles of spirits, 9,000 bottles of porter, and 500 bottles of sherry (so the story goes), he turned his attention to making a showpiece of his estate. Contemporary reports suggest that he succeeded brilliantly. But when he died, he inexplicably willed Middleton in equal parts to each of his nine children. This virtually ensured that it had to be sold.

From then on, the story was one of gradual decline. One owner, a Mr. Adams, became so Welshified by the mood of the place that he changed his name to ApAdams (the Welsh equivalent of "MacAdams"), but made no attempt at further development. After World War I, speculators moved in, and finally, during the Depression, the county council took over, dividing the land into smallholdings, logging off the trees, and putting council tenants into the remaining buildings. The location of Paxton's plantings and the details of his parks were forgotten.

This was the state of affairs when Wilkins came into the picture. A displaced Welshman himself—in 1970 he bought back the family castle of Carreg Cennen, a few miles from Middleton, which had been sold some years earlier, and moved there from London in the 1980s—he had been active in raising money and public interest in saving old gardens in South and West Wales. Middleton was very much in his mind when he heard his friend Sir Ghillean Prance, the director of Kew, comment that it was "a scandal" that Wales had no national botanic garden. Before long, a steering committee had been formed, and Wilkins found himself talking up the project to a vast number of people, from government officials to businessmen. The site was clearly choice: absolutely clean air (although pollution exists both to the north and the south); a mild, essentially maritime, climate; a range of soil types, without extremes, and useful rock outcroppings; plenty of moisture, including wetlands for aquatic and semiaquatic plants; exceptional road access, with a major motorway nearby (but invisible); and above all, a landscape of remarkable beauty and historic interest.

Things moved forward very rapidly. Every public authority in the region offered support, with the absolutely indispensable inclusion of the Carmarthenshire County Council, the owner of Middleton: for a peppercorn annual rent, it gave the project a 999-year lease. Sir Norman Foster, the leading British architect, offered a spectacular design for what would be the world's biggest botanical glasshouse, an oval dome more than two hundred yards long and one hundred yards wide, to be built into the very hilltop where Paxton's mansion had stood. Hundreds of specialists—botanists, lawyers, surveyors, historians, archaeologists, horticulturists—volunteered their services. And against stiff competition (more than 550 other detailed proposals were in the running), the Botanic Garden won a grant of £21.7 million from Britain's Millennium Commission, which hands out National Lottery money to important schemes that can celebrate the end of the century.

The end of the century, however, is less than four years away, and Wilkins has a lot to do. Walking across the rough wet grass beside him, with no sign of glasshouse or any other construction less than a hundred years old in evidence, you can't help wondering whether this may not all be a figment of an obsessive's imagination. But the plans say otherwise. As of a week ago, Wilkins has a tiny brand-new office of his own and a full-time assistant. A director, a horticulturist, and a finance director are on staff, building contracts have been signed, and construction will begin shortly. If all goes well, the glasshouse—eventually to contain five different African climates, with trees up to fifty feet high, fronted by a series of terraced cascades descending into Llyn Uchaf

(South Lake)—will be finished in 1998. So will a number of other important features (a waterside educational laboratory, a "hands-on" educational concourse called a "Bioverse," three of the restored lakes, various Welsh habitats, nursery greenhouses, and a biomass power station). Everything else—a science building; the restored walled garden together with its own antique glasshouses; a museum; the rest of the lakes and historic cascades; a complex dealing with the medicinal use of plants and centering on the activities of the fifteenth-century Physicians of Myddfai, a group which practiced herbal medicine on the nearby Black Mountain; miniature forests planted with trees native to particular regions from Szechuan to New England; two model working farms, one eighteenth century and the other modern; and much more—is scheduled for completion by 2000. In May of that year, the National Botanic Garden of Wales will open formally.

Partly by the very fact of its being new and starting from scratch ("It's a *tabula rasa*," Wilkins notes happily), the Botanic Garden can take advantage of the most up-to-date thinking on aims and procedures. It will, for example, devote itself largely to conservation, building plant collections that are as diverse genetically as possible. While its main area of concentration will be Wales and Welsh flora, including threatened species, it will also specialize in invasive alien plants, hardy ferns, water and water margin plants (there are plans to form Europe's largest collection), temperate trees from around the world, and alpines.

Much as William Wilkins cares about all this—and he does! he does!—as we plowed through the underbrush and clambered over toppling walls, I couldn't help suspecting that his real love may be Middleton, and seeing it restored to something like its original grandeur is what draws him on. Until recently, this enterprise was extremely problematic, because documentation about early plantings and layout simply did not exist. Extensive research failed to turn up anything at all. Then he had a stroke of luck. In the course of tracking down descendants of Sir William Paxton, now scattered over the face of the earth, investigators came upon a bird's-eye view of Middleton painted in 1815 by one Thomas Hornor. It was apparently part of a whole portfolio commissioned by Sir William, all the rest of which had been stolen. But this one showed everything: the lakes, the trees, the chalybeate (mineral) spring bath, the bridges and walks and drives. With such a precise guide in hand, Wilkins now has a fair chance of accurately restoring the landscape of Middleton as it existed two hundred years ago, thus creating a historical counterpoint that no other botanic garden in the world, however splendid, can boast.

Postscript: Much to his dismay, shortly after this piece was written, William Wilkins was forced to give up the directorship of the Botanic Garden project for health reasons. He remains deeply involved in several other Welsh garden restoration projects, however, and Middleton is moving ahead on schedule.

THE SHOW GARDEN

❀

One cool sunny Monday morning, Pat McCann stood on a blacktop walkway in London's Chelsea and watched as a group of men and women with clipboards and very serious expressions prowled through the garden he had built.

Miraculously, as if challenging nature's timetable, almost everything in the garden was blooming: the bluebells and daffodils scattered among the trees, the billows of yolk-yellow genista, the ceanothus and foxgloves and clematis. Even the tightly rolled irises—'Jane Phillips' and 'White City'—were slowly unfurling in the warmth of the sun. Scarcely a leaf was out of place or inappropriately wrinkled. The garden was perfect, supernaturally perfect, a garden deliberately designed and planted to look its best precisely now, on the morning of May 20, 1996, when the Royal Horticultural Society Chelsea Flower Show judges would see it.

For McCann, who is head of the School of Garden Design at Merrist Wood College near London, this moment was the culmination of nearly a year of work and worry. From the time in late June the year before, when officials from the Marie Curie Cancer Care charity approached him about building this garden in their name, his reputation had been on the line.

Putting together a show garden for Chelsea is in many ways the toughest challenge any designer can face. McCann has done it four times, in the process winning four medals. But it's never easy. You have to come up with a fresh theme, you have to devise a design that makes a strong and immediate impression, you have to concentrate on plants rather than falling back on "hard landscaping" for effects, and most of all, you must have the garden ready, at the peak of perfection, for the show itself. "Still," says McCann, "it's every designer's dream to exhibit a garden at Chelsea. It's a matter of tradition and history and recognized high standards."

When he volunteered his services—and those of a group of his Merrist Wood students training in garden design and construction—the deadline for submission of initial plans to the RHS selection committee was almost upon them. Most people have two or three months; McCann found himself with a week. His brief, moreover, was fairly specific. The Marie Curie charity wanted to include a number of plants used either in the production of anticancer drugs or in a diet to reduce cancer risks. The garden itself was intended to be a place of tranquility, not simply at Chelsea, but in reality at a Marie Curie hospice where it would be moved after the flower show was over.

With no knowledge of the site he might get, McCann went for "the ideal space": flat, big enough to accommodate the required plants, and yet capable of making an impact. In August, his design passed the first phase of RHS screening, and he was tentatively allotted a real site. It turned out to be smaller by some thirty square feet and on a one in four slope! This necessitated redesigning the entire garden. But the final screening committee okayed the new plan, and McCann was on his way. The competition had been fierce—fifty plans were submitted, only twenty-five accepted, and some thirteen kept on the waiting list in case there were dropouts.

McCann was lucky in having assured funding for his garden—the Marie Curie people had raised money from several companies as well as their own donors—because a show garden can be a very expensive proposition. Some designers have been known to go out scavenging for the money they need, which depending on the scale of the project can be as much as £100,000 ($165,000). McCann's chief problem, at this early stage, was the same as it would be later: finding plants of the right size and quality that could be made to bloom at the right time.

His initial plan called for plenty of flowers. Although Merrist Wood College has greenhouses and nurseries, they tend to concentrate on shrubs and foliage plants, so much of what was needed would have to be bought in. About six hundred plants of roughly thirty species would go into the garden. Because there was no way to be sure just which ones would be usable, however, McCann's preliminary plant list had forty species on it, ranging from *Acer palmatum dissectum* to *Vitis* 'Brant', and included a dozen or so specified by the Marie Curie director of research. Two Marie Curie volunteers, both amateur but knowledgeable plantswomen, offered to help locate suitable specimens, and in October set off touring nurseries all over southern England carrying McCann's plant list.

Eavesdropping on a meeting at the end of November between McCann and his two plant hunters, I quickly got a sense of the kind of problems they faced. He wanted a ceanothus with clematis growing through it, for example, but the hot summer of 1995 had pushed ceanothus so hard that growers were finding blooms on them already in November. By spring, there might be no blooms left. Another problem was choosing good herbaceous plants in winter, when "they are just sitting there looking miserable." Yet if the team failed to make a choice and reserve them, they might be left with nothing but "rubbish" by the time of the flower show. Very few growers will give you a guarantee of bloom. "In the end," remarked McCann gloomily, "you just have to work with what comes off that truck at Chelsea."

Plant by plant, they ticked off progress. Seed for the *Allium caeruleum* turned out to be "like gold dust"—but they found five packets, to be sown at the college. The birches might be difficult. They needed a big *Betula jacquemontii* and a *B. pendula*, both preferably potted ("Hell of a lot of money—£200"). Many suppliers don't pot, but rootball. "We'll manage," said McCann. David Austin had agreed to donate the roses, but they still had to be ordered to avoid confusion. Nobody had seen a *Hebe rackaiensis* that they were impressed with yet. They might have to settle for a 'Baby Marie' instead. And so on, through the *Salvia officinalis* 'Purpuracens' ("A funny old plant. It can look wonderful or possibly not") to the *Viburnum plicatum* 'Lanarth' (which could pose a problem flowering for Chelsea, although McCann wasn't worried). The castor oil plant (*Ricinus communis*) requested by the Marie Curie researchers presented a particular difficulty, because one supplier maintained it didn't exist!

The daffodil is the official flower of the Marie Curie Cancer Care charity—they encourage mass plantings all over the country—so daffodils had to be included in the garden. The RHS was reluctant to admit them, because they might not hold up, but McCann convinced the committee that a specialist grower could supply fine ones, and he would plant them very last thing. To provide the right setting, moreover, he would include an actual woodland, its floor covered with rough grass and forest debris and planted with bluebells. Nobody ever tried making a bluebell wood at Chelsea before; it would be a first.

McCann soon discovered one reason why nobody had done it before: bluebells can be awkward. Not that they were hard to find—the college woods were home to vast numbers of them. But the first lot of about a thousand, collected and potted up by ten husky students to be held until spring outdoors, promptly froze in their pots when the weather turned bitterly cold in December. The next batch, gathered in a January mild spell, survived well until they were all eaten by rabbits, an increasingly serious hazard for gardeners all over England.

I stopped by Merrist Wood in March to see how things were coming along. A third digging of bluebells was by this time comfortably ensconced in pots—surrounded by yards of rabbitproof wire netting—but McCann had other worries. The exceptionally cold winter had lingered on and now normal plant development had been delayed by up to three weeks. What was his impression of the situation? "One of panic." But other Chelsea exhibitors were in the same boat, even the big growers like Scott's and Notcutt's, with their special staffs of exhibition personnel and concentration on particular plants. The only answer was to juggle plants in and out of hot and cool glasshouses, and keep a close eye on them—"They can catch you out."

Oddly, a few plants were already too forward. The pulmonaria simply wouldn't have blooms for Chelsea; they were already covered with bright blue blossoms. The *Cytisus* ×*praecox*, in keeping with its name, had to be slowed down in a cool house, as did the *Ceanothus* ×*veitchianus* and the *Alchemilla mollis* ("always a difficult one"). But most plants were worrisomely slow. After being held during the winter at 15°C, the *Cotinus coggygria* 'Atropurpureus', the genista, the brunnera, and the foxgloves had all been moved into hothouses. The brunnera had responded by producing buds—too early. "I woke up last night worrying about the euonymous," McCann said. "I can't imagine why. Euonymous is usually dependable."

He figures that it is much easier to bring plants on than to hold them back. "You can blast them with heat." Sometimes, however, a plant may respond by simply shooting upwards, becoming drawn out, leggy, and sappy. "You get blooms, but the whole thing may just keel over." And with certain items, greenhouses, either hot or cold, were no help. The plan called for a yew hedge (*Taxus* is the source of an anticancer drug), which McCann had planted in long boxes. During the winter the roots froze, causing the hedge to dry out dangerously, and the only answer had been to spray it with water, even though the water was turning to ice almost in midair.

No more than a quarter of the species destined for the garden were actually present at Merrist Wood in March. The rest were being brought on by specialist growers for delivery at planting time in May. But from the number of individual plants already occupying the greenhouses, it was easy to see the practical effect of the need to have backup—three or even four times as many plants as can actually be used, so that only the most perfect specimens may be chosen.

At the start of May, with three weeks to go before the big day, the show garden itself began to take shape at Chelsea. First in was the digger, to grade the site according to plan; then, under McCann's supervision, the thirty-odd trees and saplings making up the wood at the top of the slope were winched into place and sunk into the ground, still potted.

(Like most show garden designers, McCann leaves all his plants in pots, either sinking the pots below ground level or hiding them with mulch. A favorite trick to save on expensive mulch is to inflate black plastic garbage bags part way, shove them down between the pots, and then cover them with composted bark.) Workmen poured a concrete slab for the gazebo ("They insisted on FOUR inches! You could build a house on that!"), while students began laying the stonework for the walls and hooking up the pipes and pump for the rivulet, waterfall, and pool.

With the countdown reaching three days, the detailed planting got under way at last. Hundreds of pots arrived from Merrist Wood by truck, others from various growers, piling up in large but orderly windrows of blossom to be examined by McCann and his crew. He was easier in his mind now about the condition of the plants; there would have to be substitutions (catmint and *Artemesia* 'Powis Castle' for the lavender that didn't bloom, *Euphorbia dulcis* 'Chameleon' for the astilbes), but the main plants were okay. Not for him the extreme measures forced on one exhibitor at Chelsea this year, who was spotted using a hair dryer in a desperate attempt to bring on his orchids. So far the weather was in fact on McCann's side, too—cool and cloudy, helping to hold the blooms.

As I watched, students carefully wedged the pots of herbaceous plants in place, hacking holes in the bare earth where necessary to get them at the right level. The bigger shrubs—ceanothus, the hedging, viburnum, *Cornus alba* 'Elegantissima', a splendid *Symphoricarpos ×chenaultii* 'Hancock' that had been no more than a pile of twigs two months before—already looked as though they had been there for years. So did the birches, their new foliage and catkins a delicate light green.

Sunday was the final day for setting up, with only the daffodils to be planted. A gale of wind and rain had whipped across London the night before, but fortunately no damage was done to McCann's garden. The trees stayed upright (other show gardens were not so lucky), and the flowers looked happier for the drenching. By now the bluebells were blooming in the wood where the rough grass and forest debris had been spread, and digging to hide the just-delivered daffodil pots was going on apace. McCann kneeled in front of the garden to guide the diggers in placing the clumps, while other members of the team made sure that each stem and blossom was perfect. By late afternoon, they were finished. Apart from a little nervous polishing of hosta leaves and plucking of skewed petals, there was absolutely nothing else to be done. What did McCann think of their chances? "You have to be supremely optimistic in this business."

Very early on Tuesday morning, May 21, a man on a bicycle pedaled around the walkways and avenues of the Chelsea Flower Show delivering little cards which he placed at the front of each show garden and exhibitor display that had been given a medal by the team of judges. The Marie Curie Cancer Care garden received a silver medal, third in the rank of excellence. McCann had hoped for a gold, but he was philosophical. "I thought it was one of the nicest gardens I've done. And after all, this is the Olympics of gardening. You have to be pretty pleased to get a silver." He sounded like he meant it.

V

ANTIQUARIAN PURSUITS

WATER JOKES

❧

As every parent knows, the surest way to entertain a four-year-old on an uncomfortably hot summer's day is to turn on a garden hose and let him squirt everything in sight, including himself and probably you. We've all done it. Similarly, the classic New York City hot-weather entertainment, formalized in those dandelion-head sprinklers in certain playgrounds, is an open fire hydrant blasting water over most of the neighborhood (an inverted garbage can makes it on occasion even more interesting). Water, in short, can be fun.

So far as gardens are concerned, I'm afraid, we have rather lost this instinct. We certainly don't lack for grandeur, graciousness, or beauty, and these are without question vastly worthy objectives. One has only to think of the water "eye" at Longwood Gardens near Wilmington, Delaware, ceaselessly, shimmeringly, yet almost imperceptibly overflowing; or the lake at Stourhead in Devon, brilliant with reflections in the autumn; or Brazilian designer Roberto Burle Marx's elegant formal pools bristling with jungle plants. All impressive, indeed. But fun? Not exactly.

A trip to Granada in southern Spain a few weeks ago gave rise to these thoughts. We went to the Alhambra—in fact, we stayed on the Alhambra Hill, in a one-time convent that has now been turned into an extremely pleasant hotel—to see the gardens and palaces of the Moorish kings. The Alhambra is a wonderfully watery place, especially when you think about how dry the surrounding country is. As you climb up the winding road through the woods to the palace-topped summit, a thunderous cascade emerges from beneath the walls before swirling off (invisibly) through underground conduits to rejoin the Rio Darro whence it came. This is merely the overflow, the surplus. More water fills the pools in the royal gardens and variously trickles or splashes in the fountains. The very sound of it is cooling. It's easy to understand why Mohammad ben Al-Ahmar, the Moorish ruler of this little kingdom in the thirteenth century, with arid generations of North African desert dwellers in his psyche, must have delighted in it. A lot easier, in fact, than to grasp the degree of engineering skill required to reroute an entire river eight miles through mountains in order to provide a constant flow at an altitude hundreds of feet above the plain.

The Moorish use of water in the Alhambra strikes a particularly joyful note, as if sheer abundance is itself cause for pleasure. The most charming—if not the most spectacular—part of the complex is the small summer palace called the Generalife, perched among cypresses and arcaded walks on a hill opposite the main buildings. Here you get an especially strong feeling that to the people who laid out and lived in these pavilions and gardens, water was something to *play with*. The long pool in the Court of the Canal, for example, is bordered by rows of nozzles endlessly squirting water in wobbling, chuckling arcs that mostly land in the pool, but just as often splash the stone paving and the shrubs growing in big pots alongside. The effect is whimsical. Even more whimsical—whimsy raised to a kind of art—is the flight of stairs called the Camino de los Cascades in the upper garden, with banisters that are actually narrow troughs filled with running water. I call that splendid.

The real heyday of water play in the garden was in six-teenth-century Italy. In fact, they even had a name for it—*giochi d'acqua*, meaning "water games" or (better) "water jokes." Most of the most spectacular examples have long since dried up, but a few drawings and sketches survive. More vivid are the accounts of foreign travelers, particular-ly the great French essayist Montaigne and the Englishman John Evelyn. Both men seem to have been fascinated, if not obsessed, by the tricks that could be played with water. Their journals are full of amazement.

In 1580, for example, Montaigne visited the just-com-pleted gardens of Villa Pratolino, the estate near Florence created for Francesco de' Medici, Grand Duke of Tuscany. The designer of the gardens was Bernardo Buontalenti, who on the strength of this work alone must be classed as one of the greatest hydraulic engineers of all time; he built an aqueduct three miles long and filled the place with a stun-ning array of fountains, cascades, watercourses, and pools. More than that, he showed how much fun water could be. Here is Montaigne (or rather his secretary, who was keeping notes at this point in the journey):

> There is one miraculous thing, a grotto with several cells and rooms . . . There is not only music and harmony made by the movement of the water, but also a movement of several statues and doors of various actions, caused by the water; several animals that plunge in to drink; and things like that. At one single movement the whole grotto is full of water, and all the seats squirt water on your buttocks; and if you

flee from the grotto and climb the castle stairs
and anyone takes pleasure in this sport, there
come out of every other step of the stairs, right
up to the top of the house, a thousand jets of
water that give you a bath.

The grotto at Pratolino, known as the "garden of marvels," seems to have had the whole range of water jokes: musical devices, water-powered moving figures, and tricks to play on the unsuspecting. Water played other roles too, of course; in 1645, John Evelyn reported going down "a large Walk, at the sides whereof gushes out of imperceptible pipes, couched under neath, slender pissings of water, that interchangeably fell into each others Chanels, making a lofty and perfect arch, so as a man on horseback may ride under it and not be wet one drop." Pratolino's only surviving original feature is a watery one, the gigantic statue of a shaggy bearded figure (variously called "Appenine" or "Neptune") who is squatting on a hillside apparently squeezing a cascade out of the mouth of a fishlike monster.

In Florence, at another of the grand duke's palaces, Montaigne found "a rocky structure in the form of a pyramid" containing "water mills and windmills, little church bells, soldiers of the guard, animals, hunts, and a thousand other things," all of which started clacking, spinning, and ringing when the *fontanniere* turned on the water. Mere movement was not enough. There were also sound effects. A number of gardens featured hydraulic aviaries, in which water-driven bellows produced convincing bird songs while fake birds hopped on fake branches. The Villa d'Este in Tivoli went one better, Evelyn noted. Its aviary boasted an artificial owl, and when the owl suddenly appeared, all the other birds fell silent—"to the admiration of the Spectators."

No doubt because Italy is a warm and sunny place, a typ-ical water joke usually involved a surprise drenching. Visiting Cardinal Aldobrandini's villa at Frascati, reported a dripping Evelyn, "one can hardly step without wetting to the skin." A favorite device was a stone table and stone benches fitted with hidden spray pipes, so that a too-solemn banquet could be enlivened by the turn of a tap. Pratolino had one, and an example still exists in the sixteenth-century garden of Hellbrunn near Salzburg. Given the difference in climate, the latter must have been uncomfortable.

Still more complicated arrangements for getting visitors wet amused Montaigne at the Villa Medici in Castello. His secretary described the scene:

> *For as they were walking about the garden and looking at its curiosities, the gardener left the company for this purpose; and as they were in a certain spot contemplating certain marble statues, there spurted under their feet and between their legs, through an infinite number of tiny holes, jets of water so minute that they were almost invisible, imitating supremely well the trickle of fine rain, with which they were completely sprinkled by the operation of some underground spring which the gardener was working from more than two hundred paces from there, with such artifice that from there on the outside he made these spurts of water rise and fall as he pleased, turning and moving them just as he wanted.*

Such marvels! Palisades of water springing up from the earth, a marble table "on which a fountaine plays in divers

forms of glasses, cupps, crosses, fanns, crownes &c.," mytho-
logical scenes completely animated "by the force of Water,"
storms that could be turned on and off ("with such a fury of
raine, wind and Thunder that one would imagine oneself in
some extreame Tempest"), stone musketeers shooting visitors unexpectedly with streams of water, crowns and copper
balls bouncing miraculously in midair on waterspouts,
hydraulic organs playing music all by themselves—no wonder visitors were impressed. If they were rich enough, they
went home and ordered imitations. Italian experts scattered
over Europe to supply the engineering know-how. Henri IV
brought Tommaso Francini and his two brothers to France,
where they reproduced some of the features of Pratolino in
Henri's lavish gardens at St. Germain-en-Laye. In England,
Henry VIII built waterworks at his palace of Nonsuch, and
Elizabeth I is supposed to have had a trick fountain at
Hampton Court "to play upon the ladies and others standing by, and give them a thorough wetting."

One English grotto replete with water jokes achieved
almost the fame of its Italian predecessors. Isaac de Caus, a
Dutch engineering genius, designed the gardens of Wilton
House for the fourth earl of Pembroke in the 1630s, and
when Celia Fiennes visited the grotto there forty years or so
later, this is what she found:

> In the middle roome is a round table, a large
> pipe in the midst, on which they put a crown or
> gun or a branch, and so it spouts water through
> the carvings and poynts all round the roome at
> the Artists pleasure to wet the Company . . .
> on each side is two little roomes which by the
> turning their wires the water runnes in the
> rockes you see and hear it, and also it is so con-

trived in one room that it makes the melody of Nightingerlls and all sorts of birds which engaged the curiosity of the Strangers to go in to see, but at the entrance off each room, is a line of pipes that appear not till by a sluce moved it washes the spectators, designed for diversion.

Perhaps because of plumbing problems—we must assume that at some point the taps started to seize up and the pipes to leak—or a simple change in taste, in time water jokes like these apparently went out of fashion. In 1733, the ninth earl "destroyed the old rediculous Water works and whims" at Wilton, while in 1819 Villa Pratolino itself suffered transmogrification into, of all things, an "English garden." The use of water had ceased to be playful. An odd gimmick or two lingered on—Chatsworth has a metal tree with sprays of water in place of branches. But by the end of the seventeenth century, particularly in the hands of the great French designer Le Nôtre, water in the garden had become a far more serious affair, a matter of elegance and proportion and sophistication with no interest in squirting people or making artificial birds sing. In some ways I can't help but think this a loss—perhaps a loss of innocence.

While it's unlikely that we shall soon see a return to hydraulic organs in our gardens, it would be foolish to conclude that other kinds of water playfulness are gone forever. The late English designer Geoffrey Jellicoe produced an ingenious musical cascade at Shute House in Dorset, where each tiny waterfall in the series produces a different note. Admittedly, it won't squirt you, but in my view it's a step in the right direction.

THE VERDANT CHICKEN

❧

Considered objectively, the idea of whittling large green things out of what would otherwise be shapeless trees is bizarre in the extreme. Yet that's what topiary is all about. Do you fancy a toadstool ten feet in diameter? How about a monster teapot? A corkscrew fit for an entire hogshead of wine? Or possibly nothing more than a gargantuan verdant chicken? Well, take a yew and start clipping.

It is easy, unavoidable almost, to be frivolous about topiary, especially in its remoter reaches where it consorts with garden gnomes and upended bathtubs transformed into religious shrines. Probably no other gardening practice has had such a checkered career, from admiration to obloquy and back again. Four hundred years ago, Sir Francis Bacon was declaring that "I for my part do not like images cut in juniper or other garden stuff; they be for children" (although he rather liked a "well-clippt" hedge), while much nearer our own time the great William Robinson likened it to "the cramming of Chinese feet into impossible shoes."

Often attacks on topiary were really attacks on something else—on formal gardens as opposed to naturalistic plantings, on closed-in garden "rooms" as opposed to the grand sweep of lawns, on labor-intensive gardening as opposed to low maintenance. Yet it was never quite without supporters. In spite of the savagely funny put-down by Alexander Pope in

186

his "Catalogue of Greens," in spite of the bulldozer tactics of the eighteenth-century landscape designers, in spite of the decided shortage these days of happy-though-underpaid artists with hedge clippers, topiary is still with us. We may even be in the midst of a modest topiary boom.

The principal reason for suggesting this is the current fashion for dividing up the garden and defining its structure by means of hedges. Topiary, after all, encompasses hedges of all sorts, from the simple, solid, and rectilinear through those featuring spherical or pyramidal finials to the most complicated and beswagged decorative "walls." From the last, of course, it's not a long chop to other kinds of "vegetable sculpture," if your taste runs that way.

While English cottage gardens have always featured bits of topiary, it was the so-called "old-fashioned garden" movement of the last part of the nineteenth century that brought it strongly to the fore again. This style called for "architectural" hedging featuring niches and archways, and plenty of low box borders surrounding billows of "cottagey" flowers—sunflowers, lilies, poppies, daisies. Such cultural pacesetters as the poet Dante Gabriel Rossetti and the designer–writer William Morris were charmed by topiary. On holiday in Sussex in 1866, Rossetti found a complete topiary armchair in a country garden, contrived to buy it, and transplanted it to the Pre-Raphaelite precincts of Cheyne Walk in London, where it promptly died. Morris had better luck with his yew dragon at Kelmscott Manor. He named it Fafnir and for years held a formal dragon-trimming ceremony, setting about it (as his biographer Fiona MacCarthy notes) "with large shears." According to Brent Elliott, author of *Victorian Gardens*, the popularity of this sort of figurative topiary with the general public was largely the work of nurserymen who imported finished specimens from Holland, one of whom rejoiced in the name Herbert J. Cutbush and used to exhibit "Cutbush's Cut Bushes" at flower shows around the country.

Because yew lives so long (an eight-hundred-year-old tree in a village churchyard is a commonplace—we've got one leaning over the wall outside St. Bridget's down in Skenfrith), an unspoken assumption is that all topiary must be enormously old. Age is one of its attractions. Various examples of venerable topiary in England, like the great display at Levens Hall in Cumbria, have achieved the reputation of being practically medieval. This isn't necessarily true. Elliott points out that although Levens, for example, was first laid out about 1700, upkeep of the great yew figures lapsed, and much of what's there now—looking authentically ancient, I have to say—probably dates back no further than 175 years or so. That's still pretty old, but hardly ageless.

Yet given its rap for slow growth, gardening with yew is an intimidating business. You can have a fine magnolia in two or three years, and even a laggard wisteria is going to look substantial before much more time than that has passed—but yew? Who's got 800 years (or even 175) to wait? There's no getting around the fact that yew is *the* tree for topiary—dark rich green, close-needled, easy to clip— at least in Britain where the climate favors it. Box, a close second, is no more forward.

I've been reading a little book suggesting that whatever one's opinion of the result may be, undertaking topiary is not necessarily an activity requiring two or three lifetimes to complete. The book is a reprint of Nathaniel Lloyd's *Garden Craftsmanship in Yew and Box*, first published in 1925, with an introduction by the author's famous gardening offspring Christopher Lloyd. A practical handbook to

planting, cultivating, and shaping the raw materials of topiary, its original publication gave a boost to a fashion that
had been growing since the 1880s. (It also, incidentally,
stimulated a typically explosive comment from William
Robinson, beginning "It is the poorest book that so far has
disgraced the garden." Robinson had his own agenda, and it
most definitely did not include topiary.)

Lloyd's main point—which he illustrates with frequent
reference to his own garden at Great Dixter—is that for
ornamental hedging, the common yew, *Taxus baccata*, is not
only superior to all other trees and bushes, deciduous and
evergreen alike, but "is actually one of the quickest growing
of all hedge plants, and no other responds so well to suitable
treatment." (Box is indeed slower, but has the special virtue
of needing to be clipped less often and is especially good for
miniature hedges.) The key is to choose the right sort of
infant stock and then to plant the little trees in the proper
conditions. No point in thinking about green peacocks at
this stage.

According to experiments he conducted, Lloyd argues
that the quickest results come from setting out relatively
small pyramidal plants, well branched at the bottom, in
double-dug, well-drained soil enriched with thoroughly rot-
ted manure. Three-foot specimens proved to mature fastest.
Pillar-shaped yews took much longer to fill in at the base,
and between a third and a half of the four and a half- and
six-foot plants simply died. One new hedge of three-footers,
regularly and tightly clipped, reached a height of no less
than eight feet in twelve years, with a base five and a half
feet wide! Even more remarkable was Lloyd's experience
with tiny one-foot plants, which took longer to start looking like a hedge but caught up with the three-footers in
about ten years.

Clipping, according to Lloyd, should be undertaken early in the fall—late August or during September—because growth has then virtually stopped and everything will look sharp and tidy for eight or nine months. A hedge should be cut with a batter—sloping sides—which keeps the lower parts from being starved of light. And if radical cutting is required to restore the batter, or because your yew has been allowed to get out of hand, don't worry; it can stand it.

This latter point struck me as particularly pertinent. In the last few weeks, we have visited several gardens where serious surgery on old yews had been undertaken. At Powis Castle in North Wales, a very old yew hedge had been sliced back to the main trunks along its whole length earlier in the summer; two or three months later, you could already see the new growth beginning to emerge. The same was true at *Hortus* editor David Wheeler's garden in Herefordshire, where a ninety-year-old yew hedge had to be truncated to permit a new garden plan. Frankly, I wouldn't have given this bit of hackwork much chance of recovering, but I'm now sure it will. The other example is in my own garden, where a six-foot-wide cylinder of yew makes up part of a mixed hedge otherwise consisting of hazel, privet, hawthorn, elder, dog rose, and stinging nettles. The entire top of this was inadvertently sheared off last winter by the flail mower that does farm hedges. After six months, it is sprouting nicely, covered with four- to six-inch spikes.

The existence of this chunk of yew, combined with Lloyd's chapter on "Topiary Specimen Trees," has inspired me to think that I could (before I'm too old to care anymore) create something a little more complicated and interesting than a hedge. As Lloyd says, when "treated with restraint, such clipped trees . . . provide a certain atmosphere." This may not be true of, say, a rabbit, but a turtle might be nice. Lloyd is generous with his diagrams and encouragement ("Forming birds . . . is so easily done that any intelligent person can undertake them"). He also points out that there is no reason why you can't start with something simple like a cone with a button top and let it grow into a coffee pot or a peacock—rather like carving something out of stone, only backwards.

In his introduction to his father's book, Christopher Lloyd advises the novice to "aim for broad effect and don't try to be too elaborate or clever." This strikes me as wise. The most affecting topiary, so far as I'm concerned, is not the yew man on the yew horse chasing a yew fox with a yew hound (which we saw yesterday, looking a bit the worse for wear, at Usk Castle House garden) but the black-green bulk of a sheared yew hedge backed by the bare branches of a winter tree against a white winter sky. I'm shaken by the very thought of it.

PURSUING THE PICTURESQUE

❧

*"I like a fine prospect," said Edward, "but not
on picturesque principles. I do not like crooked,
twisted, blasted trees, I admire them much more
if they are tall, straight and flourishing. I am not
fond of nettles or thistles or heath blossoms."*
   Marianne looked with amazement at Edward.
   —Sense and Sensibility *by Jane Austen*
             (1811)

A few miles west of the old town of Ludlow in Herefordshire, the River Teme flows through a gorge
choked with trees and shrubbery. The scene appears to be
utterly wild, a place where the hand of man, much less gardener, cannot have disturbed the natural confusion of
foliage and rippling water, distorted and shattered branches,
tumbled rocks and dripping moss. Gazing into the depths,
you know without seeing them that badgers and foxes must
be at home here, as appropriate to the setting as the buzzard
soaring silently overhead.

Hard as it may be to believe, this is a garden, an important one. Of course it has changed over the course of the
two hundred years since it was first created, but not as much
as you might think. In fact, if he were still on hand to lead

us through his ruined grotto for a sudden view of the river or over one of the three rustic bridges (now gone, alas), Richard Payne Knight might well feel that time and neglect had done little to damage Downton in any essential way. The wildness, the irregularity, the sense of mystery that seems to permeate the landscape would be familiar to him and welcome.

Knight meant Downton to be revolutionary. A comfortably situated country gentleman with a taste for the arts and scholarship, he had inherited the estate—ten thousand acres, along with a good bit of money—when he was only fourteen, even before going on the obligatory grand tour to Italy. Returning from the Continent, filled with enthusiasm for the villa gardens he had seen and for the paintings of artists like Salvator Rosa and Claude Lorrain (he later formed a distinguished collection of Claude drawings), he set about designing and building a castle to live in. Typically, it was unusual—imitation gothic on the outside, with turrets and parapets and interiors by improbable contrast in the grand Roman style. Even more unusual was his concept of the way the grounds around it should be landscaped.

For several decades, the reigning and all-powerful genius of British landscape design had been Lancelot "Capability" Brown. Scarcely an estate owner with a few hundred acres to his name could be found who had not already paid Brown or one of his followers to sweep away the old terraces or knot gardens, dam up lakes, and scatter clumps of trees across miles of empty lawns. ("I very earnestly wish I may die before you, Mr. Brown," an acquaintance is supposed to have said to him. "Why so?" Brown asked. "Because I should like to see heaven before you had improved it.") But by the 1770s, murmurings of discontent were beginning to be heard. This was the moment Knight began work on Downton, apparently determined to stay as far away from Brownian principles as he possibly could. Where Brown was smooth, he would be shaggy, intricate where Brown was grandly spacious, emotionally complex, even violent, where Brown was bland. Above all, his garden would be "picturesque"—that is, it would duplicate, so far as possible, the effects he admired in the paintings of his favorite artists.

From descriptions by sometimes disconcerted visitors, we know a bit about what Knight achieved. For example, in 1782, a young lady named Anne Rushout noted that "the walk afterwards brought us over a lawn where every Nettle and Thistle grows undisturbed, there were a few Rose trees just around the House but every weed had an equal share of the soil." Others were more favorably impressed, especially by the dramatic vistas Knight had carefully opened through the trees and into the gorge, and by the way he had "enriched" the natural scenery with "caves and cells, hovels and covered seats . . . in perfect harmony with the wild but pleasing horrors of the scene."

We may also look to Knight himself for a notion of what he was doing at Downton. With some (although minimal) justice, he regarded himself as a writer and had already produced books on several arcane subjects (including one called *The Worship of Priapus* on the role of the penis in pagan religion), when in 1794 he published *The Landscape*, a long poem in heroic couplets. Its basic intent was to demolish Brown (who was by then no longer around to defend himself) and Brown's principal follower, Humphry Repton, but in passing he dropped a few hints about his own approach to garden-making. These consisted very largely of, to use a famous and frequently attacked phrase from the poem, "counterfeit neglect."

What Knight seems to have meant by this was that the garden designer should aim to create scenes that matched in reality those painted landscapes by Salvator and Claude, complete with ruined buildings and broken trees and other wildly picturesque appurtenances that conveyed a sense of dramatic antiquity. But it had to be done subtly, by means of "art clandestine, and conceal'd design." The aesthetic excitement inherent in such natural phenomena as a cascade or a precipice should be preserved by the designer, although possibly enhanced by some delicate vista-cutting or path-making. In any event, you should never show your hand. Nature was the best judge in the end: "Teach proud man his labor to employ / To form and decorate, and not destroy / . . . To cherish, not mow down, the weeds that creep . . ."

The Landscape got a decidedly mixed reception. A writer in the *Monthly Review* even suggested that certain sections "lead us to suspect some intervals of poetic derangement." The poet Anna Seward detected a subversive note in Knight's overfondness for nature, "which must soon render our landscape-island rank, weedy, damp, and unwholesome as the uncultivate savannas of America." But an unstoppable tide was running in the new direction. Eccentric as Knight's opinions may have seemed to many people, they were echoed and amplified in another book published in that same year of 1794 by a second gentleman gardener, who coincidentally lived in Herefordshire only a few miles from Downton.

Uvedale Price, author of *An Essay on the Picturesque*, had been the dedicatee of *The Landscape*. He and Knight—before they both broke into print—must have spent many evenings together talking over their shared enthusiasm for landscape design and art. (They later fell out.) Where

Knight was passionate but vague in verse, however, Price stuck to prose. He was also more precise about the whole subject than Knight had been and slightly more conservative.

Price's career as a garden aesthetician had started badly. Almost his first act on inheriting his estate of Foxley a couple of decades earlier had been, "in an unthinking moment," to demolish the old formal gardens there, with their topiaries, beds, and parterres. As Christopher Hussey, author of *The Picturesque* observes, Price spent the rest of his life regretting it. As had Knight, he traveled in Italy, studied the favorite painters, and concluded that Capability's suave bareness was boring and wrong. In his mature view, "All types of gardens must be judged by universal principles of painting." But this did not entail trying to copy paintings or falling back on "unembellished nature." It was much more a matter of understanding and employing the *methods* of painters. Massing forms for structural effect, manipulating light and shade, making discreet use of color or shape— these were the tactics garden designers should make use of, whatever the scale they worked on.

In later essays, Price got more specific, discussing such subjects as "artificial water" and the way its edges could be adorned with shrubs, and "decorations near the house." Unlike Knight, he did not argue for barely cooked nature; he could see the virtues in avenues and even suggested planting climbing vines against walls and over rocks. Given that at the end of the eighteenth century horticulture had been almost totally divorced from landscape design, Price had little to say for or about flowers—except in drifts along banks, growing naturally—but his implication that handsomely planted terraces and formal gardens close to the house were not only acceptable but desirable opened the way to their return from purdah. Luckily too—because this was exactly the time when the wholesale introduction of new species from distant corners of the globe was about to begin in earnest.

Picturesque, however, was the word of the day. A Yorkshire clergyman named William Gilpin had for years been making an extremely good thing of it, traveling around the country locating and describing authentic picturesque scenes and writing influential books about them; he eventually published no fewer than eight richly illustrated volumes. (Among Gilpin's dicta: the most picturesque animal is a cow, and "Cows are commonly the most picturesque in the months of April and May, when the old hair is coming off." Dying or blasted trees are "the very capital sources of picturesque beauty.") Writers like Jane Austen and Thomas Love Peacock joked about it, while architects reached for picturesque irregularity in their plans. The Age of Reason was giving way to the Age of Romance.

Poor Repton, as the standard-bearer of the old school of landscape design, hardly had a chance. Disdained by Gilpin and attacked by both Knight and Price for too slavishly following Capability Brown, he attempted to defend himself, sputtering that "propriety and convenience are not less objects of good taste than picturesque effect." More significantly, he gradually altered his own practice, and before long was introducing elements of the picturesque in his design schemes. If these did not include Knight's "weeds that creep," they did involve terraces and formal gardens, and plantings that at least hinted at what William Robinson and Gertrude Jekyll would achieve—with a vastly expanded repertoire of flowers and shrubs—seventy-five years later.

Knight too seems to have moderated some of his more extreme ideas as time passed. He granted that the house itself needed a comfortable setting, and argued for Italian-style "terraces and borders intermixed with vines and flowers"—a far cry from blasted trees. He gradually tired of life as a bachelor in a castle, and in 1809 moved to his house in London, retaining only a cottage at Downton. The estate became the property of his brother Thomas, a distinguished pomologist and later president of the Horticultural Society.

It is possible that Thomas preferred apples and pears to landscape gardening. In any case, the first picturesque garden gradually, inexorably, returned to its wild state, not having very far to go. Today, appropriately, it is a nature reserve.

HOSEPIPES AND HYDROPHILES

❧

A few years ago, not long after I first arrived in Britain, I wrote a piece about how wet it is over here. Every time you poked your head out of doors, it seemed, the skies opened. You could figure on four or five days of gloom each week, punctuated by the odd rainbow. The whole business had an upside, of course—lush green lawns, herbaceous borders to die for. But God it was depressing.

Today we have moved to the other extreme. In this land of brollies and Wellingtons, very little rain is falling. There is dire talk of long-term climate change, drought, creeping desertification. Reservoirs are emptying, water shortages are cropping up all over the place. And while there's no reason to despair, the fact remains that the last two or three years have been the driest in Britain for two centuries—the driest, that is, for about as long as anybody has been paying attention.

Apart from acting as though Judgment Day has arrived, most British gardeners have not yet taken any serious steps toward facing up to the consequences of a brand-new climate. The assumption appears to be that you can always sprinkle your faltering hydrangeas or give the lawn a good soak. That many parts of the country have already suffered restrictions on the use of hoses—what the British call hosepipes—in every one of the last half dozen summers has so far failed to dent such optimism. But you do have to wonder whether nonchalance may be misplaced when Thames Water, one of the biggest of the regional water suppliers, issues a free booklet, prepared in conjunction with Kew, recommending the use of yucca, sage, and cacti in place of traditional English hydrophiles. Last year Severn Trent Water went so far as to suggest gardeners consider paving over a bed or two.

Possibly because of my experience of American summers (although not in the really dry parts of the country), the prospect of drought here still seems pretty remote to me. The taps are still running at Towerhill Cottage. I'm more engaged by the question of how water, assuming you have it, gets moved around the garden. Few aspects of horticulture over the centuries have had quite so much ingenuity applied to them.

These days, for example, we rather take for granted the convenience and light weight of plastic hoses. They have their drawbacks: in cold weather, coiling one is a gymnastic feat, while kinking and splitting happens all too readily. But consider the alternatives. Without a hose of some kind, it's basically buckets and muscle power. When I lived in Hong Kong, our house was on a hillside above a valley full of market gardens. I remember watching farmers trotting through fields of vegetables with pairs of sloshing pails suspended from carrying poles across their shoulders, simultaneously watering two rows and developing a permanently stiff neck.

For a long time, gardeners have been doing their best to avoid this. Irrigation channels were one solution; another was a wonderful array of "machines" designed variously to carry, spray, or pump water where it was needed. In 1577, Thomas Hyll wrote in *The Gardener's Labyrinth* of a "great Squirt of tin" that looked "like a small cannon" and could fire a fine spray a considerable distance. It did, however, take "mighty strength" to operate. Simpler devices were barrels on wheels, sometimes huge and horse drawn, and occasionally fitted with hand pumps. One eighteenth-century version had booms extending on each side with many small sprinkler heads, enabling a groundskeeper to water a fifteen-foot swathe of lawn at a pass. Of course, somebody had to keep filling it up.

As private gardens became more common in Victorian times, hydraulic invention hit its stride. Cowings & Co. of Seneca Falls, New York, came out with a magnificently be-scrolled iron "barrow engine" capable of carrying upward of a hundred gallons of water, with a pump and what looks like a firehose nozzle attached. Also available was a "watering and rolling engine" that combined a heavy roller with a perforated sprinkling bar, the whole weighing at least 150 pounds (empty). On a slightly smaller scale (in size, not versatility), there was a combination "conservatory engine and watering-pot" by means of which you could either sprinkle, syringe, or "throw a continuous stream of water a distance of about 40 feet!" That's a damned fine watering pot.

But ordinary watering pots—or cans, as they began to be called—received a lot of attention during this period too. It was probably their finest hour. The shape and size of the rose (which probably comes from the French *arroser*, meaning to water) was the first subject of debate; the gardening writer J. C. Loudon argued to some effect in favor of an inverted oval rose, on the principle that it would produce a finer spray and fall more gently. As for the can itself, English gardeners had been complaining for years that French designs, with a single hoop handle going from the side clear over the top, were better than the usual British variety with two separate handles, one for carrying and one for pouring. The solution arrived in 1886, when John Haws of Clapton in north London patented a beautifully balanced new two-handled design of such practicality that its descendants (now in a choice of plastic or galvanized steel) are still being sold all over the world.

I'm pleased to report that I have a Haws can; it holds about a quart of water and has a choice of roses. But it isn't the sort of thing you'd want to use to soak a magnolia or sprinkle a lawn. For that you need a hose. The first hoses were made of canvas or leather and had obvious drawbacks: quite apart from leaking, they were prone to rot. (Even so, leather hoses were still being sold as late as 1871, canvas hoses until the 1930s.) A greater problem was the lack of water pressure. Until the advent of public piped water supplies delivered under pressure, no sort of hose, leaky or otherwise, was of much practical use. Consequently, before the middle of the nineteenth century, hose development was more a matter of interest to firemen, whose tanks had pumps, than to gardeners.

By then, however, technology had moved ahead. Hoses were being waterproofed with various substances, including gutta-percha (from the sap of a Malayan tree) and eventually vulcanized rubber; the patent for the vulcanizing process, invented in the 1840s, expired in 1858, bringing rubber into wide use. One James Lyne Hancock invented that indispensable accessory, the hose reel. So generally acceptable did hoses become that *The Villa Gardener* magazine was moved to declare: "We do not advocate the general watering of gardens, unless there is a provision for doing it otherwise than by hand." Even so, given the cost of rubber and the natural conservatism of gardeners, it was another forty or fifty years before hoses became a gardening commonplace. In the meantime, other equipment filled the gap, such as the sensationally unwieldy French *tuyaux à chariot*, consisting of a series of metal pipes linked together and rolling about on little wheels.

The twentieth century has seen a whole range of advances in watering technology, from lightweight plastic hoses to perforated soak-hoses to underground computer-operated systems capable of doing everything short of plucking tomato hornworms. Sprinklers are a special category. Given the American insistence on trying to create English lawns in the absence of English rainfall, it is hardly surprising that they were originally an American idea. According to garden historian Brent Elliott, the first sprinkler was patented by a Buffalo man in 1871, to be followed in time by a bizarre array of swinging, spinning, oscillating, and even crawling devices, all driven by water pressure and bearing such names as "Pluviette" and "Dewplex." Personally, I swear by an anonymous gizmo with an oscillating bar that covers a rectangular area roughly fifteen by thirty feet (or possibly a lot less, depending on whether the Joneses down the road happen to be using water at the same time). At Towerhill Cottage it is strictly for soaking vegetables and flowers, however; the lawn must take care of itself. And so it will, I suspect, in spite of all the talk of impending drought.

Which is not to say that I'm wholly unconcerned about a change in the British climate. The increase in sunshine is pleasant, but I'm just beginning to get the hang of gardening here, and I'd prefer not to have to give up and start over cultivating cacti. Therefore, because our hoses and buckets and watering cans are in pretty good order, we have decided to take steps to make sure there is something to put in them. We are drilling a well, just in case.

Postscript: No well. Two bore-holes, each 250 feet deep, turned out to be dry.

MAZES

❦

A few weeks ago, English maze-builder Adrian Fisher opened his newest creation to the public. Located in rural Oxfordshire, it covers no less than six acres, contains 3.73 miles of paths, and even with a map, can take up to four hours to negotiate. Visitors are supplied with flags on long poles that they can wave if overcome by panic or exhaustion, though in utter desperation you could crash straight out, ignoring all paths. The latter move is possible because the maze is actually composed of standing field corn (which the British call maize), now roughly eight feet high. However, as the whole thing cost £10,000 ($16,000), Fisher has done his best to discourage such a move by including raised viewing platforms and signposted emergency exits.

Unlike most of the labyrinths Fisher has designed, the maize maze is strictly temporary. In a couple of months the corn will be harvested, putting an end to the maze. The idea for it came from America, where a fad for such field sports has seen the construction of dozens of increasingly grandiose puzzles in the past four years. (Fisher himself was responsible for the previous record holder, a 3.01-mile job built near Detroit in 1996.) This is all a departure from garden maze tradition, though perhaps not as great as that experienced in Japan, where vast wooden mazes (with moveable panels to add to the confusion) offer addicts a chance to scrabble at identical plank walls for many hours at a time.

As garden features go—and whatever else it may be, it is more often than not a garden feature—the maze has an exceptionally long and curious history, possibly a couple of millennia, depending on when you start counting. There seems to be some peculiar corner of the human psyche that enjoys getting lost, and the pleasure is multiplied by the knowledge that it won't be permanent. Sooner or later, you are bound to find the way out—or at least that's the theory.

Apart from the legendary labyrinth built to contain the Minotaur, early mazes were not really meant to deceive or baffle, but simply to form a decorative or magical pattern. Ancient examples that have been found carved or scratched on stone, and later ones that have survived cut into turf or laid out in tiles or colored paving in churches and other buildings, apparently served ritual purposes. While they looked complicated, and often incorporated religious symbolism, they were, as a rule, easy—if sometimes laborious—to navigate.

It was only with the development of great private gardens, starting in the Renaissance, that the possibilities for the maze as entertainment began to be recognized. Probably the world's most famous maze—and Britain's oldest surviving example—is the hedge maze at Hampton Court Palace. Originally planted—possibly replanted on the site of an earlier maze—as a minor part of the revamping of the gardens there by William III in about 1690, and since imitated more than a dozen times all over the world, it remains among the first mazes whose only point was fun.

Although quite a few of the 750,000 fun seekers who cram the Hampton Court maze each year might claim otherwise, it is not all that easy to get lost in. Technically, it is a "simply constructed maze," because the compartment serving as the "goal" at the center of the maze is part of one unbroken hedge starting at the perimeter. This means that by keeping one hand—either the right or the left—touching the hedge as you move forward, you will infallibly reach the goal, though it may take quite a while. To get out, you just reverse the process. The only problem is being patient and remembering the rule.*

A classic account of what can happen when you don't occurs in Jerome K. Jerome's 1889 comic novel *Three Men in a Boat*. The egregious Harris, after dismissing the puzzle as simple ("it is absurd to call it a maze"), declares that all you need to do is keep on taking the first turn to the right. "We'll just walk round for ten minutes and then go and get some lunch." Some time later, his confidence unshaken, Harris is deeply lost in the maze, along with dozens of mutinous and frustrated followers who had innocently thought he knew what he was talking about. ("Harris said that he couldn't help feeling that, to a certain extent, he had become unpopular.") In the end, an experienced keeper has to rescue the entire crew, including a young keeper "new to the business" who had managed to get himself lost too.

Allowing for a degree of exaggeration here, mazes like Hampton Court are meant to be difficult. It was apparently the second Earl of Stanhope, a mathematician, who came up with a couple of refinements in maze design that made them a good deal more so. One was to detach the periphery wall from the inner walls, creating "islands" inside the maze.

---

*For a quicker trip in and out: turn left on entering, then right, right again, left, left, left, and left. Now you are at the center. To get out, do the reverse.

The hand-on-the-wall method would no longer work, since it would take you right back to where you started. Such a maze is called "multiply connected." Another refinement, demonstrated in the still-surviving maze Stanhope designed at Chevening in Kent in 1802, was the absence of dead ends. You may be on the wrong path, but you will not be forced to retrace your steps from a cul-de-sac. As one writer on mazes observes, "this can give a wonderful and yet spurious sense of elation and progress."

To increase the difficulty yet more, a maze must go three-dimensional, and incorporate bridges or underpasses. Some of the best mazes feature these; the world's biggest permanent hedge maze, opened at Longleat in Wiltshire in 1978, has no fewer than six wooden bridges and a number of spiral junctions, while the hedge maze at Leeds Castle in Kent climaxes in a ninety-foot-long tunnel leading back to the outside world. Such modern creations—many of them the work of a British maze-building outfit called Minotaur Designs, of which Adrian Fisher has been a partner—are a far cry from the classic versions typified by Hampton Court. A "Beatles maze" incorporating a yellow submarine, a maze in the form of a cyclopean footprint (with a pond in one toe), a dolphin-shaped maze (in St. Petersburg, Florida), mazes depicting locomotives, dragons, and eggs—all these exist for the puzzling, if you care to look. Fisher's maize maze, incidentally, has been designed to suggest a gigantic windmill.

The craze for maze building in the last twenty or thirty years means that most of Britain's hedge mazes are modern. Even of those that trace their history to famous antecedents, very few are truly old. Like the topiary at Levens Hall in Cumbria, they have had to be replanted after their shrubberies either died or were abandoned to grow out of control.

A fairly heroic example of retrieval from abandonment is the yew maze planted in 1838–40 in Bridge End Gardens in Saffron Walden in Essex, during another heyday for maze building. This was maintained for over a century but finally given up for lost in 1949. By 1983, when a conservation group decided to try to restore it, the site was a jungle of elm and ash saplings and overgrown yews. But careful excavation and analysis of tree rings, plus the discovery of an old diagram, enabled the team to pin down the exact original design of the maze and replant it after clearing the ground. They were even able to determine just when the first baby yews had grown large enough to be shaped into hedges more than one hundred years ago.

In Britain's mild climate, yew is the classic maze material, being easily clipped, relatively slow-growing, and dense enough to deter shortcuts. But other species serve too. In the garden of the Governor's Palace in Colonial Williamsburg, Virginia, for example, a maze imitating Hampton Court has been planted in American holly (*Ilex opaca*). Privet is popular, particularly evergreen varieties. The Hampton Court Maze was itself originally planted in hornbeam. As gaps occurred, they were apparently filled in—deliberately or otherwise—with a piebald array of privet, berberis, and holly. In the 1960s, despairing curators replaced the whole lot with yew.

Today, if Hampton Court is an example of the antiquity of mazes, it is unfortunately also an illustration of their mortality. It is looking seriously tatty. Some of the yew has died and much of the rest appears to be distinctly unwell. The problem seems to be twofold: too many visitors and too little space left between the trees when they were planted thirty years ago. Palings and bits of wooden fencing are now all that prevents the development of new and radically unofficial routes.

What to do about this is not obvious. At the moment, historians are studying maze documents in the palace archives, while the garden caretakers debate whether it makes sense to patch or to start all over. It's a puzzle. Under the circumstances, Adrian Fisher ought to be grateful. At least he knows where *his* maze will be come winter—feeding a cow.

AMERICAN WEEDS

✤

I realized to my surprise the other day that I have been try-ing (and incidentally failing) to grow an American Garden. It is no big deal—at the moment it consists only of a mountain laurel, an azalea, and three high-bush blueber-ries. All are alive, but just barely, having been retrieved from the brink of terminal chlorosis more than once with a heavy dose of Miracid.

When I installed this collection on the edge of the larch wood a few years ago, I did so with nothing more than nos-talgia in mind, and possibly the happy memory of eating blue-berry slump in the New England Berkshires. That the plants (like me) were American natives passed through my mind, but it never occurred to me to make anything of it. And although I recognized that they all preferred acid soil condi-tions, that too seemed to be purely a matter of accident.

I now learn that what we've got here is at least the nucle-us of a garden type that for more than a hundred years, start-ing in the late eighteenth century, played a role of some importance in British horticulture and garden design. At the beginning, the American Garden was at least partly responsible for bringing home the blossoms so high-hand-edly banished by the great landscaper Capability Brown; in its later life, it saw the vast and colorful development of rhododendron and azalea culture. By that time, of course, it was scarcely American at all, but a motley mixture of plants from all over the world unified mainly by their common hatred of lime.

The earliest American Gardens were made to accommodate species coming in from the New World—kalmias, azaleas, rhododendrons, and low ground covers like wintergreen (*Gaultheria procumbens*), cassiopes, and bog rosemary (*Andromeda polifolia*). All of them seemed to like peaty, boggy, acid earth; there has been speculation that the first explorers, traveling along river valleys, naturally came upon such plants there. (As mountain laurel [*Kalmia latifolia*] is mostly found on hillsides in low mountains, I question this theory, but I haven't got a better one to offer.) Seeds and plants gathered by American naturalists like John Bartram, working largely along the Eastern seaboard from New England to Georgia, had been flooding into England, to be snapped up by connoisseurs. So many American plants were available by the 1760s, in fact, that Sir William Chambers could speak derisively of "American weeds" when attacking the work of Capability Brown.

It was Brown's successor Humphry Repton, however, who made a real virtue out of the "weeds." Repton realized that many of his clients enjoyed flowers, provided they could be brought back into the landscape scene in an interesting fashion. That the term "American" still had overtones of the savage or wild did no harm in those days around the turn of the century when the taste for the picturesque ran strong (see p. 192). So where Brown had depended mainly upon sweeping—and empty—expanses of lawn studded with trees for his effects, Repton was prepared to add excitement in other ways. These included separate smaller gardens that could be enjoyed independently, and many of them—as at Woburn Abbey, Bulstrode, and Ashridge—

were American Gardens. (At Ashridge, Repton actually proposed building fifteen different gardens, among them a winter garden and a medieval monk's garden, in addition to the American Garden.)

As the availability (and fashionability) of New World plants spread, other designers followed suit. The nursery-man Lewis Kennedy of Hammersmith built American Gardens at several estates in the home counties. At Fonthill Abbey, his vast and killingly expensive estate in Wiltshire, the eccentric William Beckford made what he called an American Plantation above the lake. It featured a large collection of flowering American trees and shrubs such as magnolias, robinias, liquidambars, azaleas, and rhododendrons.

Although at first they were not very interesting—mostly unexciting shades of pink or mauve—rhododendrons were destined to become the stars and the nemesis of the American Garden. Peter Collinson had introduced the first American variety in 1736, the Carolina rosebay (*Rhododendron maximum*), planting it in his garden in London, and more followed. Somewhere around the 1760s or 1770s (reports differ) *R. ponticum*—not from America but (probably via Portugal) the Black Sea coast of Turkey—opened its gross purple blooms in England for the first time. *R. catawbiense* (actually an American species closely related to *R. ponticum*) arrived in 1809, not long after a yellow-flowered variety, *R. caucasicum,* from (obviously) the Caucasus. The American Garden was becoming international, a process encouraged by the discovery that crossbreeding among rhododendron and azalea species was relatively easy, and could produce spectacular results.

In Belgium, growers crossed American azaleas (especially the pinxter flower, *R. nudiflorum,* whose pink blossoms on leafless stems in a bare early spring Appalachian wood are such a poignant sight) to create a wide variety of so-called "Ghent" azaleas. Then, in 1820, crossbreeding of the rhododendrons proper took off in earnest with the introduction of the first in a long series of imports from East Asia, R. arboreum, with massive blood-red blooms. Soon plant breeders were successfully tinkering with the whole range of characteristics—size and form of bloom, fragrance, flowering schedule, hardiness, and, above all, color. The Rhododendron Era, the era of display, was at hand.

It rather overwhelmed the more modest concept of the American Garden, even though as late as 1843 J. C. Loudon was proposing an American Garden as part of his design plan for Coleshill in Berkshire. But it has to be admitted that Loudon, for all his fame, was not an innovator. What passed for an American Garden during Victoria's reign tended to involve almost anything suited to acid soil—lilies, various conifers, heathers—no matter where it came from. Gradually, the term itself fell into disuse and vanished.

Rhododendrons and azaleas, meanwhile, found their way out into extensive and often garish plantings, encouraged by the import of still more exotic varieties from the Himalayas, China, Tibet, Japan, and the rugged no-man's-land of Upper Burma. An unassuming mountain laurel or bearberry, or even a perfumed sheet of trailing arbutus, was scarcely a match for a valley full of Lionel de Rothschild's brilliant Exbury azaleas or a copse aglow with one of George Forrest's rhododendrons from Yunnan. (He single-handedly introduced more than three hundred species.) You can see what I mean by visiting, for example, the long deep combe lying behind Lydney Park in Gloucestershire on a day in late May, when the hybrid rhododendrons are in all their blinding glory.

Perhaps it's misplaced patriotism, but I rather regret this development. It would be nice to bring back the American Garden, at least in a small way, and I'd do it myself if I could figure out some way to acidify our good red Monmouthshire clay. For that matter, I can think of a number of plants that would fit in nicely without demanding acid. I don't insist on rhododendrons anyway, and we already have our supply of R. *ponticum* that came with the house.

We should note in this connection that rhododendron fanciers—at least the eighteenth century ones—have something to answer for. *Rhododendron ponticum*, so hopefully introduced 250 years ago, has now become a simple British weed. Its leathery leaves and purple blossoms are smothering hundreds of acres of irreplaceable heather moorland from Surrey to Snowdonia. You can hardly kill it; most animals refuse to eat it (reportedly, only llamas are willing). The National Trust has gone so far as to institute a *ponticum*-destruction program. My R. *ponticum* hasn't smothered anything yet, but I'm keeping an eye on it.